CONCILIUM

Religion in the Seventies

CONCILIUM

Religion in the Seventies

New Series: Volume 1, Number 9. Sociology of Religion

THE PERSISTENCE
OF RELIGION

Edited by

Andrew Greeley and
Gregory Baum

Herder and Herder

1973
HERDER AND HERDER NEW YORK
815 Second Avenue
New York 10017

ISBN: 0-8164-2537-x

Cum approbatione Ecclesiastica

Library of Congress Catalog Card Number: 72-3947

Printed in the United States

CONTENTS

5

PART II
BULLETIN

Editorial

IT HAS always seemed to me as a sociologist that much of the theological writing on the so-called secularization phenomenon has left much to be desired. Many theologians, I think, have been all too eager to proclaim the existence of religionless man even though there is precious little sociological data to confirm that existence. There can be no objection to theologians using sociology as one of the "inputs" for their theologizing but the sociologist may be pardoned for wishing that theologians would be more sophisticated about the complexities and ambiguities that social research uncovers, particularly social research about religion.

The present issue of *Concilium*, the first one put together by a team of sociologists, is a multidisciplinary attempt to facilitate communication between sociologists and theologians. Appropriately enough, the issue is devoted to the question of the persistence of religion and calls strongly into question the more simplistic secularization models.

Most theologians, however, have moved beyond the simple, inner-directional evolutionary model of mankind moving from the sacred to the secular that characterized some theological thought in the 1960s. The function of this issue, then, is not so much to persuade theologians that religion persists as to point out the multiplicity and complexity of religious persistence. The sacred and the secular, the religious and the profane, are not opposite poles of an evolutionary model, but alternative dimensions of reality which interrelate with one another, and interpenetrate each other in complex periodicity. Van Iersel finds this

7

periodicity even in the inter-testamental era, and Baum and Brothers, in the most strictly sociological articles in this issue, argue persuasively for the complexity of the relationship between the secular and the sacred.

Religion turns up in strange places: in the scientific enterprise, according to Tracy; in political radicalism, according to Ruether; in the quest for emotional maturity, according to Kennedy; and in the complex psychological process of achieving sexual identity, according to the McCreadys. But it also continues to turn up in relatively traditional places, such as in man's quest for the mystical (Marty), and in the astonishing persistence of popular piety (Laurentin). Finally, the most primitive and archaic religious forms are not at all absent from the supposedly industrialized, secular society (Remy and Servais). While Christians may at least be happy that religion is not obsolescent, they are not committed to the proposition that the religious is not automatically good (Power) and must evaluate religion in terms of the Christian message. The great religious challenge of the time for Christians is precisely the reinterpretation of that message as we move through a difficult period between the first naïveté and the second naïveté (Shea). The McCreadys' vision of the androgynous Christian may very well be taken as the goal of Christianity as it persists through our complex religious era.

It is to be hoped that this issue of *Concilium* contributes to the development of a dialogue among the various disciplines concerned with religions—particularly theology, sociology and psychology—a dialogue in which none of the participants will be satisfied with textbook simplifications.

Gregory Baum and I worked together on the preparation of this issue. We decided that for purposes of administrative efficiency we would alternate in assuming senior responsibility for the execution of the issue. I therefore am signing the editorial of this issue and Gregory Baum will have senior responsibility in our joint enterprise next year.

ANDREW GREELEY

PART I
ARTICLES

Gregory Baum

The Survival of the Sacred

I. The End of Religion Predicted

THE disappearance of the sacred has been predicted by some of
the great sociological thinkers for over a century. Auguste Comte
held that religion would eventually be replaced by science. His
famous law of the three stages proposed that the primitive explanations of the universe in religious terms were succeeded by
philosophical theories which in turn were to be replaced by scientific knowledge. Comte formulated an attitude of mind that was
to become widely spread not only among intellectuals but among
many sectors of society. Ordinary people in an almost unreflective
way began to take for granted that religion and science were irre-
concilable and that science's victory over religion was inevitable.
This view has often been called positivism or scientism. It should
be added, however, that as a sociologist Auguste Comte was
keenly aware of the social function of religion. He was firmly
convinced, as popular positivism is not, that without a commitment to a high ideal, transcending present reality, summoning
men to altruism, sacrifice and generosity, society cannot survive
for long. For this reason Comte devised a new, rational religion
for the scientific age, one in which the object of worship would
be the future state of man, i.e., the destiny of the human race.
What Comte overlooked, according to the critical remark made
by Emile Durkheim in 1912,[1] was that religion is never a con-

[1] E. Durkheim, *The Elementary Forms of the Religious Life* (New
York, 1965), p. 475.

scious construction of men: religion happens. It is generated by life itself. None the less Comte's naïve description of a rationally constructed religion was based on an intuition which turned out to be prophetic. For the future and destiny of man was indeed to become, as we shall see, a focal point for religion in the twentieth century.

The second sociological theory for the disappearance of religion was that of Karl Marx. Marx looked upon religion mainly as the product of man's alienation. To the extent that men were freed from economic oppression and the concomitant forms of dehumanization, religion would give way to a realistic understanding of social life. For Marx religion was a form of false consciousness. It mystified the actual relationships of power and exploitation. The weakness of Marx's position was that he had never undertaken a sociological analysis of religion: the only model he used was a religion that directed man's energies to a heavenly world. It is hard to know how Marx would have reacted if he had encountered a religion that provided a this-worldly asceticism and a transcendent yearning for the transformation of earthly life. It was Max Weber, more than any other sociologist, who proposed the view, several decades after Marx, that religion was the only power that enabled men to redefine the meaning of their lives and hence had enormous potential for radical social change. Weber's entire theory of social change was based on charism and prophecy. What became clear through Weber's work was that while there was indeed religion that reconciled men with their alienation—and who would deny that many strong supporters of the Churches in various countries today desire this kind of mystification—there were also moments in history when religion made men impatient with their alienation and enabled them to transform society.

The third famous theory predicting the disappearance of the sacred is associated with Max Weber who, at the turn of the century, confirmed the suspicions of many sociologists who preceded him. Weber feared that the modern world dominated by technology and bureaucracy would inevitably limit the breadth of human experience, reduce man's awareness to pragmatic concerns of efficiency and bodily comfort, and eventually create an organized, integrated, fully planned society, the iron cage. Technocracy, so Weber feared, would weaken and ultimately destroy the great human passions, the poetic imagination, love of beauty, heroic feeling and religious experience. He referred to this sad development as "the disenchantment of the world". Religion was destined to disappear. Max Weber's theory resembles that of Auguste Comte inasmuch as both sociologists diagnosed an inevitable conflict between religion and modernity and predicted the victory of the modern consciousness over religion; but the two theories are diametrically opposed in the sense that the disappearance of religion was attributed by Comte to the liberating and enlightening effect of modern science and by Weber to the pedestrian and utilitarian preoccupations produced by the scientific world-view. Weber's theory has profoundly influenced secular and religious thinkers alike. Many people of the twentieth century have come to foresee the end of religion not as a triumph of human reason but as a symptom of the sickness implicit in excessive rationalization.

Despite its wide acceptance it should be noted that Weber's theory has never been demonstrated. The theory expressed his personal feelings in regard to modern society rather than the results of specialized studies. Weber never undertook a full-scale sociological analysis of technology. Occasionally remarks of his even suggest that the modern, rationalized consciousness pushes men to ask questions about the possible over-all meaning spanning the various human enterprises.[2] Weber's mood of despair over the modern world, so different from the attitude of his predecessors Comte and Marx, was closely related to the more recent cultural pessimism, endorsed by existentialists and Freudians, according to which society is the enemy of personal freedom and self-realization.

II. Survival of Religion Assured

The three theories predicting the disappearance of religion were not verified by the events of the twentieth century. The sacred survived. In fact, as Andrew Greeley has shown, there is not even empirical evidence for the decline of religious commit-

[2] "Science as a Vocation", *From Max Weber*, ed. Gerth and Mills (New York, 1958), pp. 143-4.

ment and attendance at worship.[3] It may well be, as some social thinkers have proposed, that religion in one form or another is an abiding human phenomenon. "There is something eternal in religion," writes Emile Durkheim, "which is destined to survive all particular symbols in which religious thought has successively enveloped itself."[4]

Religion, according to Durkheim, is grounded in man's experience of society. Durkheim, a moderate positivist himself, refuted as empirically untenable the view that religion is an imaginative theory explaining the riddles of the universe and hence would be replaced by scientific knowledge. And while the French sociologist did not deny the ideological factor in religion, he showed that historically religion has been connected with the production of culture and science, i.e., with the evolution of man, and hence could not simply be reduced to ideology. We may add that Durkheim had little sympathy for the psychological theories that sought to explain religion in terms of unconscious projections corresponding to various psychic needs. For him religion was generated by forces operative within the human community below the level of personal need and aspiration. It was inevitable, Durkheim tried to show, that men should encounter the transcendent in their lives, seek to surrender themselves to it and desire to serve it in some way or other. Religion was men's encounter with the social matrix, out of which they came to be. Religious experience, therefore, brought men in touch with their basic energies, burst the horizon of their personal consciousness, and created powers of love, dedication and sacrifice in them. (It should be added that Durkheim regarded himself as an atheist for he held that the object of worship while transcending the individual did not transcend the human community as a whole. Religion was society's encounter with its own deepest roots.)

Durkheim realized, as much as Weber, that his contemporaries, especially those formed by modern institutions and experimental science, showed little interest in the traditional religions of the West. "The old gods", he wrote in 1912, "are dying or already dead, and others are not yet born."[5] Traditional religion no

---

[3] *Religion in the Year 2000* (New York, 1969), pp. 31–73.
[4] *Op. cit.*, p. 474.   [5] *Op. cit.*, p. 475.

longer corresponded to the social experience of modern men. Would religion survive? While Durkheim was quite certain that the society resulting from the present transition, whatever it was to be, would generate religious experience and religious symbols, he did not know what this religion would be. It was possibly an element of his own theory that limited his imagination in this regard. For central in Durkheim's understanding of religion was the radical distinction between the sacred and the secular, a view that since then has often been criticized by anthropologists. And as we shall see, the religious vitality of the present age has challenged this view within the Christian Churches. But whatever the limitations of Durkheim's imagination in regard to the future, it is reasonable to ask the Durkheimian question today: What are the manifestations of religion in the present and what is their relationship to Western society?

III. THE GODS OF TODAY

We must note, first of all, that there are geographical areas and sections of the population where the traditional forms of Christianity have resisted the challenges of modernity, critical scholarship, ideological critique, humanitarian influence, etc. There the Churches symbolize the people's attachment to a past cultural or political age. They even attract the support of men with little religious feeling yet committed to the defence of the old order. The ideological component of this kind of religion is only too obvious. It is no accident that the fundamentalist and evangelical Churches in the U.S.A. are conservative and sometimes reactionary political forces. The same may be said of groups within the Catholic Church resisting the renewal movement. In many so-called Catholic countries the Church still stands for values, institutions, and a view of authority characteristic of the baroque age. Conservative Catholics in the more secularized parts of Europe are deeply attached to a certain refined form of culture that is threatened by present developments: their religion is connected with a certain "Europeanism", not quite as unabashed as Hilaire Belloc's, but just as inveterate. Here the sacred survived much longer than Weber and Durkheim had foreseen. It should be added, of course, that these remarks in no way question the genuine character of this conservative piety: all that is claimed is that this piety corresponds to a past experience of society and hence has built into it trends that seek to preserve as much as possible the institutions and the power relations of those days.

Of greater interest to us in this article is the present crisis of Western religion—as clearly visible as the cultural crisis—and the new religious phenomena. We shall mention the widely spread interest in the occult and in Eastern meditation, and finally, as the most significant development, the discovery of the religious dimension of historical humanism.

The surprising interest in the occult among a considerable section of the population, especially young people, has been widely noticed and frequently discussed in sociological journals. Many of the gods exorcized by Christianity a long time ago have come back to life. Among many students who at one time wanted to be known for their critical spirit, we find a fascination with the cultic, with worship and ritual, prayers and incantations, the use of incense and drugs, etc. We observe the cult of the irrational in certain religious movements concentrating on Jesus or other religious personalities. We find this cult in more bizarre forms in astrology, witchcraft, devil worship and the like. Since the new interest has created a market for enterprising business men, the cultic practices, or, at least, voyeuristic interest in them, have spread very widely among people, while the authenticity of these rites has become somewhat questionable. For many people the occult has become a game, sometimes a terrible one.

The religious significance of this new interest, even where it is sincere, is minimal. It is significant only as a symptom of the present cultural crisis. The new devotion to the occult seems closer to magic than to religion. In the terminology of Max Weber, the magical focuses on *ad hoc* interests and particular problems of the clients, with no further impact on their personal lives and on society as a whole, while the more specifically religious relates the worshippers to powers operative in the universe, and hence tends to order their personal lives and have an impact on society. The great religions, according to Weber, were powerful, culture-creating movements. When the German sociologist after World War I faced a generation of students fascinated by the occult, he denied that their practices contained anything sociology recognizes as religion.[6]

At the same time the turn to the irrational is a significant protest against the highly rational, technological and bureaucratic society of the West and as such deserves to be taken seriously. This point has been repeatedly discussed in the pages of *Concilium*.[7] It is worth noting that this protest is tainted by a good deal of "resentment". Those who react to, and seek to overcome, the unhappy split between reason on the one hand and the bodily, emotional and spiritual aspects of life on the other, are often, because of resentment, unable to turn to the creative elements of their own tradition, which challenged this split in the past: they turn, rather, to elements that are culturally so far removed from them that they can never be integrated into their lives. It is this sort of resentment that makes the turn to the irrational often such a self-damaging thing.

Distinct from, though culturally related to this interest in the occult is the new interest in the spirituality of the East.[8] A great number of intellectuals, especially students, have turned to the contemplative traditions of the East, adopted ancient practices of mental concentration and bodily posture, reject the modern world as a harmful illusion, and through contemplation and a new life style seek access to the really real. This movement has made available in inexpensive editions the wisdom books of the East and produced its own literature as well. While this pursuit of Eastern wisdom may be rewarding and liberating for those who follow it, it is not, in my view, a significant religious development. It remains a private cult, a parenthesis within the present culture, symbolic of its crisis, but not a focus of spiritual power re-ordering cultural values and affecting the vision of society. Contemporary intellectuals are so deeply formed by modern life and its recent past that they are unable fully to enter the symbolic world of the East, assimilate it creatively and make it a principle of social life. The modern question for Eastern

[6] *From Max Weber, op. cit.*, pp. 154–5.
[7] Andrew Greeley, "The New American Religion", *Concilium*, Nov. 1971 (American Edn., Vol. 69).
[8] Cf. David Bradley, "The Western Crisis and the Attraction of Asian Religions", *Concilium*, Nov. 1970 (American Edn., Vol. 59).

contemplation will remain a private adventure, possibly magnificent, with a minimum of social impact.

Of greater social significance, though numerically possibly quite small, are the new conversations between Christian contemplatives and the religious men of the great Eastern traditions. The sociological impact of religious dialogue, under certain favourable conditions, has been amply demonstrated in the twentieth century. In such conversations between East and West, the Christian may be able to relate the elements he learns from others, especially if they offer a corrective for his own immediate culture, to various aspects of his own religious tradition, bring the Eastern symbols closer to the symbolic language of the West, and take steps to integrate the contemplative strains of the East in a vision of society that is realistically grounded on the Western past. Not every mysticism is viable. Even the mystical life of the few, if it is to be creative, must be related to the symbolic world of the wider society.

IV. The Religious Focus

I now turn to a religious phenomenon found within the Christian Churches as well as among people who have moved to the margin of the Churches or have abandoned Christianity altogether. The phenomenon I wish to describe is very common indeed, though it is not always understood in religious terms. It is often expressed in secular language. The phenomenon creates a special attitude to the world and leads to certain kinds of action so that it appears to many as an expression of humanism. What has emerged in the Western world, under historical pressures and spiritual influences, is a new self-experience of humanity producing powerful feelings of solidarity with other people, especially the underprivileged, and a powerful sense of being destined to a higher life. This is the self-experience that Vatican II referred to with approval as "the birth of a new humanism, one in which man is defined primarily in terms of his responsibility for the brothers and for history".[9]

While these experiences of solidarity and common destiny are

[9] *Gaudium et Spes*, n. 55.

indeed secular, they have a religious dimension to which people are sensitive in varying degrees. Solidarity and common destiny are overriding convictions for many people, lifting them out of the social framework in which they find themselves, making them cross the boundary lines they have inherited, bringing them in touch with values that transcend them and their own communities. For the sake of these values they are often willing to make sacrifices, give up their personal comfort, contradict the authorities at some risk, and take upon themselves a heavy burden they could have avoided. Thus they feel enlarged: they recognize themselves caught in a life that is not their own. These deep convictions make people see their life and history in a new light and supply them with a hope that makes the present struggle worth while. Such people know themselves to be face to face with a reality that has no name, yet to which they are committed.

Contemporary religious experience has shown how inadequate and misleading is the strict separation of the sacred and the secular. For what is characteristic of this age is that people encounter the sacred as the deepest dimension of significant secular experiences, namely the pivotal points of their history, personal and social. There is religious meaning in man's vocation to become fully human.

In the following paragraphs, I wish to concentrate on the social dimension of humanization, even though there is religious meaning also in man's personal transformation. Solidarity, I contend, cannot be accounted for simply in moral terms; it implies conversion or change of consciousness. For the experience of solidarity with all men, especially with the disadvantaged, makes us sensitive to the manifold forms of oppression operative in the world; it demands that we open ourselves to the full extent of evil in human life, recognize that these forces are operative in our own lives and societies, and admit that greater humanization will be available to men everywhere only if we ourselves and our societies are willing to change. The contemporary experience of solidarity is different from the optimistic universalism of nineteenth-century liberalism. This universalism, even when it was religiously based, wished to extend the values and advantages of the privileged society to the whole world. The present experience of solidarity brings out more clearly the evil operative in contemporary culture, leads to a critical review of inherited values, and creates a desire for social change. It is this aspect of conversion or change of consciousness that gives solidarity its religious dimension.

Nor can the experience of common destiny be reduced to purely moral terms: it includes both faith and hope. For men are profoundly touched not only by the conviction that human life is not as it ought to be but also by the unaccountable faith that human life is meant to be different, that it is up to us, to people, to transform it, and that by doing so we follow our call and destiny. Not only is the world incomplete, damaged, fragmentary, it is also oriented to a higher, freer, more human way of being. This destiny summons us to act. While it is possible to interpret this experience (as well as that of solidarity) in a purely secular way, many people are sensitive to a dimension in this experience that is specifically religious. For man's vocation is not man-made. Man encounters his destiny; he discovers it, receives it, is addressed by it, marvels at it, and makes it the ground of his hope.

This religious experience of man's vocation, I contend, is widely spread and of great power in the present age. Even when solidarity and the common call are not interpreted in religious terms, their expression in literature, films and modern songs usually betray religious overtones. Those who want to express this experience spontaneously turn to religious symbolism. For vast numbers of people Jesus has become a symbol of liberation. The experience described in these pages is found especially among groups and movements that are critical of the present culture and its institutions. Young people who have rejected the institutional boundaries and values they have inherited are familiar with this experience. The new sense of man's vocation supplies the energy behind social action groups that work for changes in society, the ecological movement that tries to preserve the earth's surface, the growth movement and therapeutic groups that promote liberation and creativity among people, and the political groups that anticipate more radical changes of the social order.

This new humanism is felt very deeply within Western religion, in the Churches and Synagogues. Because of it, people

have often moved to the margin of their Churches; sometimes
they have even left the Churches when these refused to respond
to the new sense of man's common calling. Yet this is not all.
While solidarity and the common vocation seemed at first to be
at odds with traditional doctrine and action, the new religious
experience has profoundly affected the life of the Churches themselves. It has led Christians to understand the message and call
of Jesus in a new way. Theologians have re-read the Scriptures
and the ancient Christian authors and found that the new experience corresponds to valid aspects of the Christian tradition.
While these aspects were marginal at one time, in changed circumstances and under the influence of new religious experience,
they have become central. They have today become the focal
point for understanding the Christian message. Eventually the
Churches have come to review their stand and to adopt the new
viewpoint in their official teaching. At Vatican Council II the
Catholic Church declared itself in solidarity with mankind, engaged with other men in the common calling to transform life
on this earth, and trusting that the mystery of redemption, operative in human history and revealed in Jesus Christ, appoints all
men to liberation and reconciliation. It is my view that the vitality
of the Christian movement in the West is largely built on this
new religious experience.

At this point we recall the Durkheimian question. What are
the new religious manifestations to which the society at present
in the making gives rise? We have examined the popular interest in the occult and in Eastern meditation on the part of an
élite, and found that these do not manifest the signs of religion
in the Durkheimian (or the Weberian) sense. They are not
grounded in social life. They are inspired by social resentment
rather than by an identification with a social movement. They
are "gods of the moment" without much power. However, the
new religious experience of man's humanity, so widely spread
among diverse groups, has shown remarkable social vitality and
become a source of renewal within the Christian Churches. Here
is the sign that points to the future development of religion.

With Durkheim we must ask the question: What is the social
basis for this new religious experience? This basis, it seems to
me, is the global community that is in the making. Man's life

on this earth is being unified through a common technology, new means of communication and transportation, the intercontinental web of science, commerce and industry, the common threat to human survival, and the vulnerability of the whole earth to a disaster taking place in any one part. Mankind today suffers from common problems and seeks common solutions. The revival of ethnic consciousness, a surprise to many sociologists, may well be caused by the fear that the world population is endangered by a trend towards uniformity and the loss of particular traditions. The return to ethnic consciousness may therefore be a sign that the global community is in fact in the making. We note, moreover, that the new ethnic consciousness as well as contemporary religion have no imperialistic designs: they promote a spirit of solidarity and co-operation with others as long as the survival and vitality of their particular traditions are guaranteed. The common fate of men on this earth has become an overriding fact of life. Here is the social basis for the religious vitality of the future.

The religious experience of man's vocation is closely related to the creation of small communities, a social phenomenon examined in the present issue of *Concilium*. These communities wish to become matrices for a more liberated human life. While they are critical of the established societies and inherited loyalties, they are not turned in on themselves. In this they differ from many sectarian movements of the past. The small communities in fact facilitate and support the religious orientation towards solidarity and man's common calling.

Andrew Greeley

The Persistence of Community

ONE OF the most striking events of the past decade has been the emergence of small group communities in the midst of Western urban industrial society. Some social scientists have told us that community was dead, that man lived an isolated anomic life as part of a mass society or a "lonely crowd". Some theologians have "celebrated" the glories of the freedom and the privacy that came to man in this lonely crowd. If he no longer belonged to anything, it was argued, he was now the master of his own fate; he made his own decisions quite independent of the social pressures of the tribe and the clan.

But while the obsequies of community were being celebrated in one part of the university campus, in another part of the campus astrology groups were being organized. Sensitivity training and marathon encounter sessions were beginning. Communes were being formed, covens of witches appeared, and before one knew it there was the extraordinary phenomenon of the Jesus people, those primitive Christians, breaking into the drug-infested counter-culture and bearing witness to the saving grace of Jesus. The old religious and tribal communities may have been dead but new religio-tribal communities were being born.

Some observers interpreted these communities as evidence of a "resurgence" of religion with either joy or sorrow, depending on their frame of reference. However, in the context of the present issue of *Concilium*, it is argued that the new communitarian movement, to the extent that it is religious, represents a persistence of religion, although obviously a persistence in a new form, a form that is not altogether without dangers.

Four different questions will be posed in this paper, firstly, how can we explain the communitarian movement; secondly, whether it is a religious movement; thirdly, the dangers of such a movement; and fourthly, how traditional churches should respond to the communitarian movement.   ·

Before we answer these questions, however, we must first have a definition of community.

> By community I mean something that goes far beyond mere local community. The word, as we find it in much nineteenth- and twentieth-century thought, encompasses all forms of relationship which are characterized by a high degree of personal intimacy, emotional depth, moral commitment, social cohesion and continuity in time. Community is founded on man conceived in his wholeness rather than in one or another of the roles, taken separately, that he may hold in a social order. It draws its psychological strength from levels of motivation deeper than those of mere volition or interest, and it achieves its fulfilment in a submergence of individual will that is not possible in unions of mere convenience of rational assent. Community is a fusion of feeling and thought, of tradition and commitment, of membership and volition. It may be found in, or be given symbolic expression by, locality, religion, nation, race, occupation or crusade. Its archetype, both historically and symbolically, is the family, and in almost every type of genuine community the nomenclature of family is prominent. Fundamental to the strength of the bond of community is the real or imagined antithesis formed in the same social setting by the non-communal relations of competition or conflict, utility or contractual assent. These, by their relative impersonality and anonymity, highlight the close personal ties of community.[1]

The Nisbet definition is certainly accurate for community as the term has been used in the past. However, today, there is frequently a new dimension added to the category "community", a dimension which is almost always present in the communi-

[1] Robert Nisbet, *The Sociological Tradition* (New York, 1966), pp. 47-8.

tarian movement and is generally present, too, when a young clergyman says that he thinks the role of the priest is to "create community". That new dimension is one of interpersonal intimacy. It is not merely required that one associate with one's "own kind of people", it is also necessary that the association be intimate; that is to say, that the relationship be characterized by so powerful and so systematic a trust that most of the masks and the defence mechanisms which make everyday life relationships tolerable if impersonal are dropped and we relate to one another with the totality of our selfhoods. Even in those communes which are not given over to complete sexual freedom, the intimacy which is supposed to exist between husband and wife is still held up at least implicitly as a model for all other human relationships.

I. WHY THE QUEST FOR COMMUNITY?

The distinguished anthropologist Clifford Geertz has argued that fundamental and primordial groups seem to be one of the "givens" of human society.

By a primordial attachment is meant one that stems from the "givens"—or more precisely, as culture is inevitably involved in such matters, the "assumed" givens—of social existence: immediate contiguity and kin connection mainly, but beyond them, the givenness that stems from being born into a particular religious community speaking a particular language, or even a dialect of language, and following particular social patterns. These congruities of blood, speech, custom, and so on, are seen to have an ineffable, and at time overpowering, coerciveness in and of themselves. One is bound to one's kinsman, one's neighbour, one's fellow believer, *ipso facto*, as a result not merely of one's personal affection, practical necessity, common interest, or incurred obligation, but at least in great part by the virtue of some unaccountable absolute import attributed to the very tie itself. The general strength of such primordial bonds, and the types of them that are important, differ from person to person, from society to society, and from time to time. But for virtually every person, in every society, at almost all times, some attachments seem to flow more from a sense of natural—some would say spiritual—affinity than from social interaction.[2]

The most popular theoretical explanation for the "resurgence" of community is that under the pressure of urbanization and industrialization the old communities have collapsed. The mass society, the lonely crowd emerged during the 1950s and the 1960s, as everyone from Ortega y Gasset to Harvey Cox predicted; but men found that the loneliness and the isolation of the impersonal mass society was intolerable. They turned to radical political movements, psychological encounter groups, new religious forms (such as astrology and the Jesus people), and counter-culture communes in order to recapture the intimacy that had been lost on the pilgrimage from *Gemeinschaft* to *Gesellschaft*. It is precisely the most lonely and the most alienated, according to such an argument, who will flock to the communitarian movement.

There is perhaps something to be said for such an explanation, but it also seems to be rather naïve, both in its romanticization of the old community and in its description of contemporary society. One very much doubts, for example, that there was much in the way of interpersonal intimacy in the old peasant village. Strong social support there was, and also strong social control, but intimacy of the sort that the new communitarians seek was practically unknown. The peasant village was not an open, honest and trusting place; it was closed, suspicious and rigid. Most of the enthusiasts for the new communes would have found the old villages intolerable.

There is an extensive sociological literature which offers convincing evidence that *Gemeinschaft* has survived and prospered in the midst of a *Gesellschaft* society. Informal friendship groups permeate factories, residential neighbourhoods, the military establishment, the market-place, and even the political order. The extended family is not nearly so extinct as many observers would like to believe. For example, more than half the American population lives within fifteen minutes of the parent of one of the spouses. The majority of Americans are more likely to visit each week with their brothers and sisters than they are with anyone else.

[2] Clifford Geertz, "The Integrative Revolution", in *Old Societies and New States*, ed. Clifford Geertz (Glencoe, Ill., 1963).

Far from there being less intimacy in urban industrial society than there ever has been in the past, there is probably more. One could make a very persuasive case that more intimacy is both possible and expected between husband and wife than in any previous time in history. The psychological breakthroughs of Freudian therapy and existential personalism makes trust and openness among friends more likely now than ever before. There may be much more impersonality in human relationships today than in the past, but there is also more intimacy. The reason these two assertions are not contradictory is that the sheer number of human relationships has increased dramatically.

Thus, the "alienation" explanation for the new communities, while it may have some merit, also misses many important phenomena in modern society. There are a number of other explanations which must be combined with the alienation theory before we begin to understand the new communes.

1. The sheer fact that men and women have more time to devote to things other than just staying alive is extremely important in explaining the quest for intimacy. You don't have time to worry about whether you love or are loved or whether you "belong" to anything when you do not know where your next meal will come from. It is precisely in the newly affluent upper middle-class that the quest for intimate communities is the most powerful. I am not suggesting that affluence causes the quest, rather that an increase in affluence makes it possible for more people than ever before to seek something besides the bread that is necessary to sustain physical life.

2. Modern psychology, with its strong emphasis on personal relationships and self-fulfilment, has provided men and women with a vocabulary that enables them to make their needs for intimacy explicit. The contemporary world of human relationships is not harsher than the world of the past, but I would argue that our expectations of what those relationships ought to be like has changed notably. Marriage, of course, is a classic example of this. The maintenance of the family property, continuation of the family line, effective working of the family farm, and the satisfaction of minimum sexual needs was enough for husband and wife relationships in a peasant society. One does not want to be so naïve as to say that there was never any depth of love between

spouses; there was indeed in many cases. The point is that the ecstasies of romantic love were not expected, and the marriage relationship could survive without them—as in many cases, no doubt, it had to. In the contemporary world, the marriage relationship is expected to provide the fundamental life satisfaction as a relationship quite independent of any other social or cultural role. One lives for one's spouse in a way that would not have been intelligible in years gone by. Men and women may very well be much more skilled in the arts of interpersonal intimacy than they were in the past, but if they have acquired both greater skills and greater opportunities for intimacy, so, too, have they acquired much greater expectations. Here is the problem not only for marriage but for all human relationships. It is not that the interpersonal ambience has deteriorated since the past; on the contrary, it has got much better. Our expectations for psychological satisfaction from human relationships have increased, and increased much more rapidly than the quality of human relationships. It is not that we are getting less out of relationships, it is rather that we expect much more.

3. Finally, in past times, men did not have options about the community to which they belonged. One was part of the group into which one was born. Only by leaving the group physically—a most extraordinary thing to do—did one exercise a choice, and that was a choice that gave no assurance that one could ever become part of another community. The immigrant was a marginal man and was likely to remain marginal for all his life. However, there is in the world today a number of options about one's primordial group. One can *choose* where one is going to belong. While from the point of view of freedom this increase of options represents an improvement, it also poses a new obligation on the human person, particularly the young human person. If one is able to choose, it is difficult to escape the responsibility of choice, and now the issue of where one chooses to belong becomes an explicit and occasionally terrifying question. Affiliation is now a matter of choice and, hence, a burden and a responsibility. One does not necessarily inherit one's primary belonging as did one's predecessors. Hence, the search for something to belong to becomes more important, and for those who lack security in their own personal worth, also more agonized.

Choice, affluence, and a revolution of rising expectations—these factors explain why many of those who drift into the new communities are not especially alienated or lonely. We are not dealing, in fact, with an attempt to recover interpersonal intimacy that existed in some mythological past. On the contrary, the new communitarian movement, however it may refer romantically to past stages in human history, represents an attempt to create something entirely new: a culture based on openness, trust and explicit affection. It is as something fundamentally new in the human condition that it must be evaluated; and to the extent that it is religious, it should be understood not as a resurgence of religion but rather as a development of a quite new religious form.[3]

II. ARE THEY RELIGIOUS?

There is considerable debate among those who are studying the new communities as to whether they are religious or secular and whether they will survive. Not a few of the debaters have vested interests in contending that the new communities are neither religious nor likely to survive. It is certainly true that most of the communities collapse after a rather brief life. It is also true that many of them are not explicitly religious (particularly the psychological encounter groups and the political communes). Finally, it is true that most of those who join communes do so only for brief periods of time and do not intend to, or at

---

[3] I am not suggesting that there was no search for intimacy and trust in past religious forms. Surely, many of the founding groups of the great religious orders were seeking—though not with such an explicit vocabulary—the same thing the new communitarians seek. The men whom Vincent, Francis, Ignatius, Benedict and Dominic gathered around them were at least for a time intimate communities. However, as soon as canon law intervened, these communities adopted an organized structure, and they lost their primitive communal forms. The rhetoric, the vocabulary and the ideology of the contemporary communitarian would strongly resist such "institutionalization". The new communitarians will argue that the Jesuits were much better off when they were a handful of men around Ignatius, and the Franciscans were much better off before Brother Elias "institutionalized" them. But the important point is not that the new community will strongly resist institutionalization; it is that the old communities would not have understood the problem in the terms that are taken for granted today.

least do not in fact, commit the rest of their lives to such behaviour.

One reply to those who deny either the religiousness or the permanence of the new groups is to assert that at least some of them are quite explicitly religious and that others, particularly the rural farm communes, have taken on a religious colouring—complete with sacramentals, rituals, purification rites, and frequently strong astrological views of reality.

While something can be said for this response, my own inclination would be to take a broader view with the observation that whatever happens to a particular group and however brief the involvement of many people may be and however explicitly religious or unreligious the communities may be, the important phenomenon is rather the widespread quest for intimacy, a quest of which communitarian movements themselves may only be the tip of the iceberg. It is virtually impossible to share the kind of trust and intimacy which contemporary personalism thinks is the highest goal of human life unless one shares fundamental values and world-view with those among whom one seeks intimacy. The quest for intimacy, I would assert, is always religious, and probably, in the long run, always sacred.

Extremely powerful psychological forces are released when one takes and permits oneself to be taken in an intimate relationship. In themselves, these forces are neutral; they can be positive or negative, constructive or destructive, but they are primordial human drives that are normally contained within systematic defence mechanisms. The openness, defencelessness and psychological nakedness involved in the quest for intimacy reveals, or at least purports to reveal, the most basic selfhood of the person. Under such circumstances, great powers of both love and hatred can be released. Whether love or hate will predominate depends to a considerable extent on whether the people involved share the same primal convictions about the nature of reality. Much of the disillusionment, disappointment and tragedy that are so frequent in the commune movement results from the fact that either common world-views are not shared or that, if they are, convictions about them are so weak that they cannot overcome the fear, the anguish and, at times, the terror that intimacy creates.

One seeks intimacy, then, with one's own kind of people because in the final analysis it is only with one's own kind of people —that is to say people with whom one shares the most profound and powerful convictions—that intimacy is possible. The commune movements call forth a religious response almost inevitably because they touch that which is most fundamental and basic in man: the core of his selfhood. The group member necessarily deals with his own primal conceptions about the nature of the Real.

The quest for community, I would suggest, represents at first implicitly and then explicitly—frequently in a quite painful fashion—the quest for a common faith to share. This faith may be an explicitly religious transcendental faith or it may simply be a view of the Ultimate without a transcendental referent. From a social science viewpoint, it matters little. In both cases, man's search for intimacy involves him willy-nilly in a search for the Ultimate.

In this frame of reference, then, the question of whether the new communitarian groups are a permanent or a transitory phenomena becomes less important. I doubt very much that any social science observer of the contemporary world doubts that the quest for interpersonal intimacy will persist. So long as men and women are seeking to reconstruct their own particular segment of the world along personalistic lines, the religious question will remain an extremely important one. If, as I have argued previously, the quest for intimacy represents not a return to the past but a beginning of a rather new phenomenon in human history, then it would follow that we are also witnessing the beginning of a new development in man's religious behaviour; an increasing number of men and women will be seeking for a religious perspective powerful enough to overcome the fears and tame the wild passions that are released by the search for intimacy. If these assumptions are correct, then it may very well be that religion is not merely persisting but is entering a whole new era, an era in which religious faith (or basic worldview, to use more neutral words) becomes the explicit basis for the creation of very new and much more intense kinds of personal relationships.

III. WHAT ARE THE DANGERS?

In a previous article for *Concilium*, I pointed out a number of the dangers of the new religious phenomenon. There are some special dangers in the communitarian component: (a) a man who seeks intimacy—at least who seeks it honestly—makes himself extremely vulnerable. He opens himself up to others, and in that act he becomes very weak in his psychological position vis-à-vis others. The man seeking intimacy says, in effect, "Here I am, trusting and defenceless before you." Only the most naïve would think that this man is not running a risk of being badly hurt. Trust is admirable, but there are also a considerable number of people whom one really ought not to trust.

When one gives oneself over in intimate relationships to a group, one is at the mercy of tremendous group pressures. It is well known that some people can be personally "destroyed" in the tough and brutal interaction of a marathon encounter group. Those who best survive such sessions are not the most honest but those with the toughest skin. Those most likely to be hurt are not necessarily the most aggressive but often those who are most gentle and vulnerable. A disturbed but vigorous person, understanding the mechanics of group dynamics, can wreak havoc on others in an intimate group setting, and a group which contains a number of such people will almost certainly create an extraordinarily dangerous situation.

In intimate groups there is a tendency for everyone to fall back on those defences against intimacy one learns in one's earliest years. Thus, intimate communities often represent simply a collective regression to childhood behaviour patterns, in which all one's partners in the group become surrogate parental or sibling figures. Under such circumstances, all the group's energy is expended in a usually fruitless attempt to straighten out the kinks of interpersonal relationships, and the attempt will never be successful precisely because it suits the purposes of many if not all of the members of the group to keep it fixated on interpersonal problems. Thereby, it need not face any of its responsibilities to the world beyond itself. The phenomenon of collective regression is really a form of psychiatric gnosticism.

Frequently the defence mechanisms that arise in such groups

to protect its members from intimacy become more elaborate and more vicious than those that are practised in ordinary human relationships. In the name of a libertarian ideology and using the rhetoric of psychological personalism, narrow, oppressive and rigid tyrannies come into being. The tragedy of the so-called "Manson family", which was involved in several murders in California, is but a bizarre extreme phenomenon that occurs not infrequently in other communal groups. The strong members dominate the weak, in the name of freedom and openness, indeed, but in fact with an oppression that is all the more dangerous because it masquerades as freedom.

In summary, intimate communities are only for those who are personally mature and psychologically sophisticated. Unfortunately, many of those who are attracted to such communities possess neither quality. Those who do possess them have no particular need to join dubious communitarian efforts. Mankind may have invented a vocabulary for *talking about* personal intimacy and increased its expectations of experiencing such intimacy, but the development of those skills which are required for *living in* community seems to have lagged behind. The search for personal intimacy is not likely to cease, despite the grave injury many people suffer in such a search. Those who embark on the search for community should be aware that it may turn out to be a very dangerous and unpleasant voyage.

IV. What does it all mean for the Churches?

It is fashionable in some religious circles to see the communitarian movement as a judgment on the churches. It is argued that young people who are flocking to the communes are searching for something the Church should offer but hasn't. They reject the Church because the Church is not living up to its own professed communitarian principles.

A point must be conceded in this argument: there can be no doubt that Jesus did demand a high level of trust and openness in those who enter the kingdom of his Father, although it must also be asserted that trust was a consequence of the grateful acceptance of God's gracious love and not a cause of it. If in the long history of Christianity more of us had believed in the Good

News of Jesus and loved one another in the confidence of our faith, there would be much more intimacy in the human race than there is at the present. But it does not follow that we can achieve instant intimacy or convert the world into one gigantic commune over night simply by an act of will. The attempts of some clergymen to become like hippies and of others to form communes in which intimacy is achieved instantaneously demonstrate theological, psychological and sociological naïveté. The growth of the human personality is gradual and organic; it cannot be speeded up by high pressure techniques. Similarly, the Holy Spirit works where he will, and our enthusiasm and energy can no more constrain him to blow whither we will than can our rigid organizational structures. The enthusiasm of some clergy for "creating community" is simplistic when it is not dangerous. If the Church has failed in the past to respect human dignity and integrity because of the rigidity of its formal structures, it can all too easily continue to fail today by misguided attempts to force highly stylized forms of intimacy on everyone, whether they are ready for it or not.

But if the churches must be wary of a false intimacy that is imposed on the instant, they should not be blinded to the importance of the personalist quest as a sign of the times. The fundamental theme of this issue of *Concilium* is that religion persists and that what may look like simplistic evolution is in fact a periodicity of alternating factors. This periodicity is not merely circular. The rhythm between church and sect is inherent in the Christian tradition. Men will alternately develop sects that are highly exclusive and then develop churches which are inclusive. The communitarian movement, both inside and outside the Church, is essentially an exercise in sect formation. But while the new sects have something in common with the enthusiastic sects of the past, with both the Montanists and the Franciscans, for example, they still represent a critically new development in the human religious pilgrimage. New sects may run the risk of gnosticism, oppression, manipulation, suffering and disillusionment; but they also represent a conscious, explicit and psychologically sophisticated attempt to love one another even as Jesus loved us. They are not a resurgence of religion; they are rather a persistence of religion, but a persistence of religion in a new, interesting and potentially productive form. Theologians would be well advised to reflect on the meaning of this quest for community, to inquire what light the Christian symbol system might be able to shed upon. Churchmen, working out of the richness of the Christian theological and communitarian heritage, should not be afraid to assume a position of leadership in the communitarian quest. Christianity certainly cannot take exception to a movement which in its best manifestations seeks to bind men together in faith and in love.

Martin Marty

The Persistence of the Mystical

THE persistence of the mystical motif in contemporary culture may not serve as a proof for the existence of God, but it does reveal much about the situation of man. In their paradigmatic projection of human and cultural possibilities, Herman Kahn and Anthony J. Wiener looked to *The Year 2000* and offered a "basic, long-term multifold trend".[1] Such a trend, many of whose origins can be traced back as far as the twelfth century, is considered relatively "surprise-free", according to these authors.

Their widely accepted model, growing in part out of the work of Pitirim Sorokin, says that cultures will become "increasingly sensate (empirical, this-worldly, secular, humanistic, pragmatic, utilitarian, contractual, epicurean or hedonistic, and the like)". While this sensate trend goes back seven or eight centuries, its progress has not been uninterrupted. The Reformation, the Counter-Reformation, the Puritan era in England, and some aspects of the Later Victorian era are in a way contradictions to the basic trend. Yet the trend remains.

Kahn and Wiener go on to report, however, that Sorokin, along with most of the nineteenth- and twentieth-century philosophers of history, envisaged some sort of "religious" stage after sensate culture. This stage could be spiritual and intellectual, properly religious, a synthesis, or "something completely different".

[1] H. Kahn and A. J. Wiener, *The Year 2000* (New York, 1967), pp. 39–48.

Not many years ago the philosophers of history were being heeded little, while the basic secular trend was being adopted. Even in theological circles and among philosophers of religion there were many attempts to suggest that not only absolutes, the transcendent and the quest for values and meanings would diminish and disappear, but even that curiosity about them would be left behind. In a world come of age, the dimensions of man and culture which pointed to wonder and mystery would be regarded as vestiges of a past that would inevitably have to be left behind. A single, all-embracing style of rationality was envisaged and set forth as exemplary.

So pervasive is the reductionist secular model for man and culture that during the period of the regnancy of secular theology it became fashionable to speak of the mysterious and mystical dimensions of humanness as throwbacks. One could relate to these almost exclusively through a kind of regression to infantile or, at best, adolescent stages of human phylogenetic development. The race was "beyond all that". Where it persisted, this survival remained only as a result of cultural lag. The mystical could live on as superstition in underdeveloped nations or undeveloped sectors of advanced societies. It was part of the primal vision in Africa, something that would certainly be shrugged off as Africa bought the dubious blessings of Western technopolitan life; it inhered in what the Eastern world wanted to forget.

Today's surprise in the world of surprise-free trend-spotters occurs as a result of the fact that the mystical aspect persists, however, not only in lagging portions of the culture but in the *avant-garde*. One looks for recovery of the mystical interest in those circles and élites where elements of tomorrow's world are anticipated today. So much is this true that serious students of the ways in which man relates to transcendence are sometimes put off by the fear that they be typed as being fashionable and faddish.

Any study of the surviving character of mystical interests finds itself preoccupied with problems in the sociology of knowledge. How does one locate the people in whom these impulses live on? How seriously should one take the mass media's concentration on a topic which they drop as rapidly as they pick it up? How does the advance guard connect with the rest of the human race?

While it is impossible and unnecessary to develop full answers to these questions at length here, it does call forth at least one cautionary word.

While noting the presence of mystical strivings in the world of youth, students, affluent suburbanites, entertainers, communicators and intellectuals, one must recognize that they may represent a statistically small sample of the number of people who in quieter and less flamboyant ways sustain the concerns year in and year out. It has been suggested that a manifestation becomes truly manifest when the sons and daughters of people in these influential circles take it up. For example, in advanced societies there have always been millions of people who relished occult phenomena. They subscribed to metropolitan newspapers which ran horoscope columns. They bought astrological readings. Almost every superstition known to man lived on in their orbits. But these represented a little-noticed sphere. When just a few more people showed interest—if these people were influential transmitters of signals and symbols in society—the larger public was notified that there was an "occult explosion". While this essay may now and then imply an interest primarily in the *avant-garde*, we are assuming that we are touching only on the edges of a larger reality.

The middle-class, mobile, relatively affluent intellectuals who turn from the simply sensate-rational-secular style to the religious and even the mystical are interesting because they are the people most free to leave behind the concern for transcendent recognitions. They are economically best poised to have control over those instrumentalities which historically, it was presumed, led people to seek contact with the divine or higher and other stages of human consciousness. Death is a remote reality in a welfare state with its social security, efficient hospitals and devices for obscuring the vision of disease from the physically healthy. One can evade many terrors simply by holding a position of dominance in a class-structure, or because of a certain status and prestige. Nature is kept at a distance, its threats minimized. Yet precisely the people who could repress the vision that has led man to seek the gods are those who account for most of the renewed interest in the mystical.

The phenomenon shows up in at least three ways. First, there is a kind of self-generated anthropological character. Something in man strives to be expressed. Some speak of this as a "rebirth of wonder" (the poet Lawrence Ferlinghetti) or a "sense of wonder" (the ecologist Rachel Carson); to others it may represent "rumours of angels, signals of transcendence" (Peter Berger) or a more profound "mystery of being" (Gabriel Marcel). In any case, it is hypothesized that man is somehow by nature a being who, when given the freedom to express himself, will do so with allowance for mystical elements.

The second revelation of the persistence of the mystical has to do with the ways in which Westerners who cannot reach into their own past for models and who have not within themselves the resources for projecting a future, reach laterally to other cultures. In these other cultures something of that to which the mystics turned survives. The experience of mass higher education, mass communications and widespread travel opportunities make access to other cultures possible and attractive. "He who never visits thinks mother is the only cook"—this Bantu saying summarizes something of the visiting that has gone on in and from the West in the recent past. As noted above, the "primitive" or "primal" world of Africa and elsewhere in the southern hemisphere has been satisfying for many. The divine is located in the tree, under the stone, in what a Westerner might see to be a kind of pantheistic or, better, pansacramental awareness.

More naturally and more obviously are the effects of fresh encounters with the East. Attractions of Zen, Tao and Hindu spirituality have reached major sectors of the culture. The East historically disdained Western linear rationality; indeed, it negated Western ways of looking at history and its meaning and purpose. Western man seeks a union with "the all" by following Eastern modes of piety.

A third form which these phenomena take might be called the way of retrieval. There are resources in the West for mystical awareness, and while the mystic may seek to transcend historical knowledge, precedent and trappings, it is possible that the climate for transcendental searching may be cultivated by historical recall of past mysticism. Some have seen this searching to be present in the rather colourful, noisy and agitated fashions which are not always compatible with serious mysticism, in Roman Catholicism's "new pentecostalism" or Protestantism's various "Jesus movements".

The stirrings may be located outside Christianity as well. In *Congress Bi-Weekly* for 28 January 1972, Rabbi Byron L. Sherwin summarized the situation in Judaism. "Especially among youth, the emphasis is upon inspiration rather than information, exaltation rather than rationalization, authenticity rather than apologetics." This "surge of interest in mysticism" is also present in Judaism. Sherwin claims that the German rationalist lineage (Heinrich Graetz and others) saw Jewish mysticism to have been only "a lunatic fringe". In America Mordecai M. Kaplan and the Reconstructionists downgraded the mystical. But despite this, and as a result of the witness of other schools in Jewish leadership, the mystical motif persists, as in the *Kabbalah*. The liturgy, ethics and *Halakhah* have many notes encouraging the mystical. Abraham Joshua Heschel, who would not be defined precisely as a mystic, has tried to show that Jewish theology embraces a polarity between rationalism and mysticism. He even goes further at times and insists "that mysticism is the essential element in Judaism, conceptually and historically". For Max Kadushin, "Judaism *is* mysticism". In making that claim he follows Evelyn Underhill's definition: "Mysticism is the act of establishing man's conscious awareness of the presence of the divine." According to Rabbi Sherwin, Jewish youth has little occasion to look for mysticism in Zen or the occult. They have only to overcome their parents' distortion of Judaism and retrieve their authentic tradition.

Many Christians are also engaged in such retrieval. They may go through Jerusalem's gateway or door—as Martin Buber speaks of it—since it stands between East and West. They will find elements of something approximating nature-mysticism in the Psalms. And while in the technical sense St Paul's approach is not mystical, they know that something quasi-mystical goes on in his 164 references to being "in Christ" (or cognates of that term). They find Paul in the desert, being transported to other realms, open to transcendence. The desert monastics, medieval free spirits and religious geniuses have come back into their own. Teresa of Avila, John of the Cross, Julian of Norwich, Meister Eckhart and Jacob Boehme are being revisited.

No one knows quite how to measure the degree of acceptance of these three and other mystical affirmations and quests. The devices for polling the public are almost too precise to be of aid here: how does one reduce to focus answers to questions such as: "Have you ever had a mystical experience?" or "Does the transcendent invite your interest and attention?" One can learn something from the best-seller lists, the growth of cells and movements, the campus concerns, the media's almost instinctual and not necessarily inaccurate appropriation of the phenomena. One need here say little more than that something is going on "out there", both in élite and in mass culture. More important may be the question: What do we seek to measure?

The present concern does not have to do with mystic achievement but with mystic awareness and aspiration; one might say that we are more interested in extraordinary experiences of ordinary man, not in those of religious geniuses. The mystical need not be confined to such geniuses, and it would be hard to enlarge the inquiry at all were one to have to content oneself with the rare flowerings of such high expression. They occur inexplicably, now and then, but in any case rarely. Since this inquiry begins with an anthropological and sociological concern, we content ourself with and even delight in evidences of the widespread character of the aspiration.

For that inquiry, the mystical search may be defined in W. Stace's term as "the apprehension of an ultimate *nonsensuous unity in all things,* a oneness or a One to which neither the sense nor the reason can penetrate". This definition is then enlarged and "brought down to earth" by the addition of Evelyn Underhill's classic version. Mysticism is:

the name of that organic process which . . . is the art of [man's] establishing his conscious relation with the Absolute. The movement of the mystic consciousness towards this consummation is not merely the sudden admission to an overwhelming vision of Truth: though such dazzling glimpses may from time to time be vouchsafed to the soul. It is rather an *ordered movement* towards ever higher levels of reality, ever closer identification with the Infinite.

Stace and Underhill are both quoted in John White's anthology of sophisticated essays on the mystical subjects, which is itself a documentary support of our thesis concerning the pervasiveness of present-day survivals of interest in this "ordered movement towards ever higher levels of reality".[2]

The White book reproduces Stanley Krippner's "Altered States of Consciousness", which classifies styles of consciousness. His list provides another anthropological clue as to why the mystical is pursued. He does not sort out good from bad altered states, but simply cites them in wild juxtaposition to prepare readers for the recognition that they need not be content with one version. The state includes dreaming, sleeping, lethargy, rapture, hysteria, fragmentation, regression, meditation, trance, reverie, daydreaming, internal scanning, stupor, coma, stored memory, expanded consciousness along with the hypnagogic and hypnopompic. Finally, the twentieth state is "the 'normal', everyday, waking state, characterized by logic, rationality, cause-and-effect thinking, goal-directedness, and the feeling that one is 'in control' of one's mental activity".

At this point dissenters against the mainline culture, sometimes exaggerating their difference from it in order to buy time to define themselves independently or in order to draw attention to the superiority of their alternatives, give some reasons for their mystical apprehensions. "What is so good about normal consciousness?" Is it not the everyday waking state that produces dehumanizing work ethics, which make life less worth living? Others say that ordinary logic and rationality produce foolhardy ventures including the computerized brutalization of the Vietnamese war. Cause-and-effect thinking, when it is left to itself, lets man arrogate to himself what ought to be left to mystery and to the divine. Goal-directedness is the property of those who project administrative mentalities that enslave man. Being "in control" is done at the expense of wonder.

So some people try to "centre" in themselves, visit the primitive or Eastern or occult religious worlds or retrieve from the Western religious past, in order to withstand the powers that would depersonalize them ever further. The ecological movement was born not only in the conscience of rational technolo-

[2] John White, *The Highest State of Consciousness* (New York, 1972), p. 155.

gists but also in the circles of poets, soothsayers, casters of spells and communitarians. The latter may have held naïve and often foolish visions of what can and should be done to preserve nature, but they have also helped awaken attempts to stimulate wonder and love for the environment.

Why do people seek "the highest state of consciousness" or contact with the infinite, the All? The first reason we have given for the persistence of the mystical, then, has been the desire to enlarge consciousness itself, ordinarily with the purpose of withholding consent from a repressive surrounding order. Another motive, of course, may be natural human curiosity about some of the nineteen alternative modes or styles of consciousness. This may represent a human desire to use elements of mind which civilization normally suppresses, to help one see how the human situation will be improved if there be different and even higher orderings.

A second reason for the persistence of the mystical inheres in the intrinsic character of the experience itself. However arduous and painful some such experiences may be, many people are driven to pursue them simply because they are available. They describe as salutary and salvific the moment which permits the ordering of reality, the appropriation of the ordinarily unaccessible. In a sense there is a kind of aesthetic defence: must one "justify" a symphony? Then if not, why must one justify a transcendent experience, since it may best signify that which makes human life worth living? "Taste and see that the Lord is good"; a "more abundant life" is promised.

Earlier reference to the fact that the new would-be mystics go visiting the Southern or Eastern hemispheres for spiritual models and resources points to a third reason for many people's advocacy of the mystical route: it provides empathy with the rest of the world. Just as it is or may be creative to go deeper into one's self in order to transcend the self, so one learns to relativize Western contemporary experience by seeking that approach to the spiritual which most humans would regard as normative. This means a kind of de-institutionalization of religion, a removal of the spiritual quest from a grim, productive, work-a-day churchly ethos. One enjoys nature, God, the other, the self on a new and different set of terms.

A fourth reason has also been implied in a different context: the mystical quest produces a sense of a bond with nature. Some types of mysticism, of course, lead the religious genius to move "outside" the world of things. But we are speaking here again of the extraordinary inside the ordinary, of the mystical route which may allow for contact with nature and the other. Martin Buber is also quoted in the White book: "To look away from the world, or to stare at it, does not help a man to reach God; but he who sees the world in Him stands in His presence . . . to eliminate or leave behind nothing at all, to include the whole world in the *Thou*, to give the world its due and its truth, to include nothing beside God but everything in Him—this is full and complete relation."[3]

Others describe their transcendental quest as being motivated by their desire to define themselves and others apart from the realm of necessity, work, professionalism and vocation. They know that in a world of expanding ease and prolonged leisure, people's worth must be measured in new ways. Mysticism allows one to "turn off the clock" for a while, and to perceive matters in fresh ways.

Implied through all these, however, is the beginning point of our own inquiry and hypotheses: that at stake is the attempt to perpetuate a richer model of man than that projected by a sensate culture. Here one encounters "the dancing God", the realm of play, the ludic dimension which is not easily embraced by technopolis and the over-administered life. Maybe a style of consciousness which transcends old definitions between the secular (which persists) and *homo religiosus* (who is going through transformation) will be creative.

No one concerned for the whole human record can observe the persistence of the mystical without expressing at the same time some concern for the directions it may take. Worst of all, it has often turned to be merely self-preoccupied, an exercise in narcissism. One seeks his or her own gratification at the expense of the neighbour's need. The whole accent falls on being aloof from social passion. Or one may generate private passions which lead to fanaticism, pride and hypocrisy. The person who has had

[3] John White, *op. cit.*, p. 293.

quasi-mystical experience is not always necessarily better for it. He or she may become presumptive, crusading, or—maybe, worse?—a bore.

Therefore many advocates of the new spirituality urge that it be sought and nurtured in a social context; one kind of mysticism calls for the self-reflective soul to be isolated in its quest. But others—one thinks of the Thomas Mertons, Daniel Berrigans, Jacques Maritains—blend social passion with various transcendent visions. J. Robert Oppenheimer fused scientific thirst with devotion to Indian spirituality. Dag Hammarskjøld was a pragmatic statesman and at the same time the mystic author of *Vågmarken.* It is possible to combine the visions and passions, and many mystics in the past—in both East and West—have done so.

It is possible that the heightened interest in persistent mysticism may represent a brief and passing phase in the modern world. Certainly many of the phenomena which are celebrated by the mass media season after season disappear from view soon after they are noticed. What is important is not each one of these manifestations, but the totality in which they occur. They suggest that individual persons and the culture as a whole have not made up their minds to follow but one style of being in the world, that the models for man and culture are richer than many people had thought, and that the quest for unification and transcendence is undimmed.

The Christian knows that his faith's future does not simply depend upon the number of people who take seriously such quests, nor does their presence assure a necessarily easier time for the faith and the Church. But the survival and even growth of a culture in which these are at home suggest that Christians would be unwise to narrow the range of human expectations late in the twentieth century; there are still surprises in the human spirit.

Joan Brothers

On Secularization

"The problem is not one of constructing definitions of religion. We have had quite enough of those; their very number is a symptom of our malaise. It is a matter of discovering just what sorts of beliefs and practices support what sorts of faith under what sorts of conditions. Our problem, and it grows worse by the day, is not to define religion but to find it."[1]

From earliest times men seem to have feared the loss of small communities. The very factor of size in itself is threatening to some. The processes of industrialization have increased concern among some social commentators as to man's fate. We can see mirrored still in the world's large cities the consequences of the Industrial Revolution, though historians have pointed out that in many cases the rural conditions from which populations were fleeing were as squalid as those which awaited them in the cities. The social theorists of the late nineteenth century and their successors were greatly concerned with the sociological consequences of the transition from rural to urban life. The concepts and typologies they developed to interpret the events experienced by Western European and North American societies exemplify their interest: Durkheim's mechanical and organic solidarity, for instance; Tönnies' *Gemeinschaft* and *Gesellschaft* or Cooley's primary and secondary groups.[2] Not all viewed urbanization as

[1] Clifford Geertz, *Islam Observed* (New Haven, 1968), p. 1.
[2] See Andrew M. Greeley, "After Secularity: the Neo-Gemeinschaft Society: a Post-Christian Postscript", *Sociological Analysis*, XXVII, 3 (1966), pp. 119–27.

a bad thing, though; the great German sociologist Georg Simmel, for example, saw that the city provided a milieu where the individual was freer to pursue his interests.[3]

But both religious and popular thinking, conscious of the appalling legacy left to us by rapid industrialization, often equates urbanization with general decline. Thus, many attempts have been made to determine the effects of industrialization on the family, seeing it as robbed of vital functions, neglecting to consider what kind of existence the families of the poor could ever have had in the impoverished rural areas they hastened to leave at the onset of the Industrial Revolution. Even without evaluation, functionalist explanations in sociology tend to see the nuclear family as directly related to the needs of industrialized societies.

In religious terms, secularization is seen as one of the consequences of industrialization. It has long been a commonplace that religion is a phenomenon to be found in all societies. It now seems to be a commonplace to assume that industrialization inevitably saps the religious vigour of a once devout people and reduces them to the general state of secularization. This view of societies as developing from a religious to a secular state provides an example of the persistence of evolutionary theories in sociology.

In the course of industrialization do societies in fact evolve from being religious to becoming secular? To whom do we owe these ideas? How accurate a picture of social reality do they present? It is with these questions that this article is concerned.

A Secular Society?

Secularization appears to most observers of industrialized societies to be a factual description of things as they are. The churches and other religious institutions seem to be confining their activities to increasingly fewer areas of life; education is a typical example in many societies. The roles and functions of religious personnel become increasingly restricted, their traditional tasks being taken over by specialist professions. Church–

[3] This whole area of concern is discussed in detail in Jacqueline Scherer, *Contemporary Community: Sociological Illusion or Reality?* (London, 1972).

State confrontations increasingly end in the retreat of ecclesiastical authorities. Everyday experience seems to confirm that organized religion is the concern and activity of only the committed few (theologians have developed frameworks to interpret this), and that secularization is a fact of contemporary life.

But everyday experience also seems to indicate that there are remarkable instances of the persistence of religious activity. In Britain, for example, while church attendance is low, studies show that very few people care to describe themselves as non-believers.[4] (This ambivalence has been satirized as "The creed of the English is that there is no God and that it is wise to pray to him from time to time."[5]) A leading sociologist of religion, David Martin, suggests that "far from being secular our culture wobbles between a partially absorbed Christianity, biased towards comfort and the need for confidence, and beliefs in fate, luck and moral governance incongruously joined together".[6]

Many would feel that there is an increasing interest in moral problems if these are defined not in terms of traditional prohibitions but in relation to sensitivity to the problem of war, hunger and poverty. There are also, from time to time, significant debates over religious issues. Thus, the philosopher Alasdair Macintyre made this comment on the controversy over Bishop Robinson's *Honest to God*: "More than one kind of raw nerve was touched by Dr Robinson's theme. For he drew our attention to the fact that although the death of God has been announced over and over again in our culture, it remains true that God is an unconscionable time adying. I do not refer by this to the staying power of ecclesiastical institutions; they probably contribute to the strengthening of atheism as much as they ever did. But the survival of religious modes of feeling and questioning at widely different levels in our culture points clearly to something that Nietzsche and Feuerbach missed."[7]

Since our common sense assumptions are so contradictory, can we accept them as valid? Should we be asking quite different

[4] This evidence is discussed in Joan Brothers, *Religious Institutions* (London, 1971).

[5] Alasdair Macintyre, *Against Self-Images of the Age* (London, 1971), p. 28.

[6] David Martin, *A Sociology of English Religion* (London, 1967), p. 76.

[7] *Op. cit.*, p. 12.

questions about the nature of religious experience in modern societies?

The sociological literature on secularization abounds, and most of it is on the theme that what we should be concerned with is the growth, extent and direction of secularization. That is—and this is crucial to the current discussion—it is concerned with the measurement and assessment of what is already presupposed to exist in society. The initial stage of uncovering societal presuppositions concerning what is meant by secularization is ignored.

It can of course be said that since many speak of secularization, it has meaning for *them* and as such is relevant to the sociological task.[8] Were the majority of sociologists who concern themselves with secularization and those theologians and pastors who follow their activities actually examining the intersubjective meanings attached to religion, then one would have no grounds for complaint. But few, in fact, treat secularization in this way, or indeed as a concept or an analytical tool. They take it for granted and construct theories upon what is in itself a reification.

A parallel can be found in the ways in which ebbs and flows in crime rates were solemnly assessed before the imaginative work of sociologists like Howard S. Becker showed that we were accepting predefinitions made according to varying criteria by other professionals and by members of society. In the case of secularization, we often accept popular or theological predefinitions of religion without asking how relevant and useful they are to the investigation in hand.

Now there are three main grounds from which one can start to criticize sociological uses of the concept of secularization and to question its value in understanding what is happening in society. These assumptions are:

1. That it is possible to demarcate clearly the territory of the sacred from the profane.
2. That primitive cultures tend to be religious while industrialized cultures tend to be secularized.

[8] See here Peter Berger's *The Social Reality of Religion* (London, 1969), originally published in 1967.

3. That religious experience is identified with participation in institutionalized religion.

Let us look at these assumptions further.

I. SACRED VERSUS PROFANE

First of all, secularization involves the assumption that it is possible, empirically speaking, to divide the world into the categories of the religious and the secular, or the sacred and the profane. Is such a typology useful? It is noticeable that some of the major exponents of the secularization hypothesis are those with least interest in asking what for the empirically oriented sociologist is always the major question about a tool or concept: *Does it work?*

Let us examine how this concept of secularization is used, and from whom we derive it. The notion of secularization is one that has been adopted by sociologists from those in other disciplines. Thus, Owen Chadwick has indicated in his history of the Victorian Church in England that although modern historians first began to apply this term systematically to the nineteenth century, the Victorians themselves used it from the eighteen-seventies onwards. He himself comments on the term: "That it represents truth is hardly to be denied, but what truth is not so easy to define."[9]

If the initial interest in the question comes from historians and social commentators, sociologists have not been slow to develop its use. In his famous exposition of an evolutionary approach to religion in *The Elementary Forms of the Religious Life*, using secondary sources on Australian totemism, Emile Durkheim argues that religion is the system of ideas which represents society to its members: "For Freud God is the father, for Durkheim God is society".[10] Religion itself, in his classification, belongs to the broader class of the sacred. The sacred consists of those things which are set apart and forbidden, the interdictions which isolate the sacred being applied to profane things. (The anthropologist Mary Douglas suggests that this opposition between the sacred

[9] Owen Chadwick, *The Victorian Church*, II (London, 1970), p. 423.
[10] E. Evans-Pritchard, *Theories of Primitive Religion* (London, 1965), p. 63.

and the profane was a necessary step in Durkheim's theory of social integration, expressing the opposition between the individual and society.[11])

Implicit in the use of such a typology is the assumption that since there are two distinct areas of life, it will be possible for one area to infiltrate the other. Whereas Christian theologians have assumed that the profane area ought to be permeated by the sacred, it is often assumed by other observers that it is the area of the sacred that will be eroded with the advances of scientific knowledge. As we increasingly understand the mechanisms of the profane dimensions of life, the argument goes, so we will have less need to resort to religious interpretations.

These assumptions were criticized on empirical grounds by the distinguished anthropologist E. Evans-Pritchard in his important general work, *Theories of Primitive Religion*. He bases his case upon the anthropological data now available. Does the ethnographical data support the Durkheimian dichotomy, accepted since by many social scientists? Evans-Pritchard doubts it: "Surely what he calls 'sacred' and 'profane' are on the same level of experience, and, far from being cut off from one another, they are so closely intermingled as to be inseparable. They cannot, therefore, either for the individual or for social activities, be put into closed departments which negate each other, one of which is left on entering the other. For instance, when some misfortune such as sickness is believed to be due to some fault, the physical symptoms, the moral state of the sufferer, and the spiritual intervention form a unitary objective experience, and can scarcely be separated in the mind. My test of this sort of formulation is a simple one: whether it can be broken down into problems which permit testing by observation in field research, or can at least aid in a classification of observed facts. I have never found that the dichotomy of sacred and profane was of much use for either purpose."[12]

In his remarkable comparative study of Islam in two cultures, the American anthropologist Clifford Geertz speaks of the methodological problems involved in defining the religious perspective; he indicates that although this is possible, it cannot be

[11] Mary Douglas, *Purity and Danger* (London, 1966), p. 21.
[12] *Op. cit.*, p. 65.

done by seeking crude indices or classifications: "We look not for a universal property—'sacredness' or 'belief in the supernatural', for example—that divides religious phenomena off from non-religious ones with Cartesian sharpness, but for a system of concepts that can sum up a set of inexact similarities, which are yet genuine similarities, we sense to inhere in a given body of material. *We are attempting to articulate a way of looking at the world*, not to describe an unusual object."[13]

Other studies indicate that there is no inevitable sharp distinction between the sacred and the profane in the ideas of the communities studied. Amongst the anthropological accounts which indicate that the religious practices of pre-industrial societies are not necessarily an alternative to or in opposition to scientific concepts is Godfrey Lienhardt's study of the Dinka. Here he remarks that the Dinka do not "expect sacrifice automatically to achieve some specific result with the certainty of a well-tested technical procedure. So they will accept medical aid at the same time as preparing sacrifices for the recovery of the sick. Medicine is not an alternative to sacrifice and prayer, but may complement it."[14]

II. RELIGION = PRIMITIVE; SECULAR = MODERN

The second assumption relating to secularization, the equating of religious devotion with primitive societies and scepticism with complex, industrialized societies, is also open to question on empirical grounds. To some extent this kind of assumption rests upon wishful thinking, the hope that with scientific advances men will get beyond religious questions. However, the secularist movements offering solutions alternative to those given by traditional religion do not appear so much as to have replaced but rather to co-exist alongside organized religion.[15]

The assumption that members of rural or peasant societies are devout is a highly questionable one. David Martin discusses the extent of religious disaffection in the seventeenth and eighteenth

[13] *Op. cit.*, pp. 96–7, my italics.
[14] Godfrey Lienhardt, *Divinity and Experience: the Religion of the Dinka* (Oxford, 1961), p. 291.
[15] See Colin Campbell, *The Sociology of Irreligion* (London, 1971).

centuries in England and Wales.[16] The work of people like Fernand Boulard and Jean Remy in France make it plain that we cannot make assumptions about rural populations being faithful in their religious observances either now or in the past.[17]

As for the view that societies evolve religiously, fundamental to the Durkheimian perspective, Evans-Pritchard had earlier attacked evolutionary theories of religion in his account of the Nuer, a cattle-herding people of the Sudan. "The Nuer", he says, "are undoubtedly a primitive people by the usual standard of reckoning, but their religious thought is remarkably sensitive, refined and intelligent. It is also highly complex."[18] Such data strongly undermine the assumption that religious sophistication is the province of industrialized man, while members of agrarian economies are content with simple views. He goes on to say that, while he accepts that many features of religion can be related to the social structure of a community, Durkheim and his followers, basing their conclusions as they did on faulty data before systematic fieldwork was regarded as an essential part of the anthropological task, went too far in their interpretations.

The most pointed attack on equating secular views with contemporary society has been made by Mary Douglas in her recent book. She relates secularism not to industrialization or any other comparatively recent trend, but to "a definite social experience which need have nothing to do with urban life or modern society". Far from secularism being the product of industrialization: "The idea that primitive man is by nature deeply religious is nonsense. The truth is that all the varieties of scepticism, materialism and spiritual fervour are to be found in the range of tribal societies. They vary as much from one another on these lines as any chosen segments of London life. The illusion that all primitives are pious, credulous and subject to the teaching of priests or magicians has probably done even more to impede our understanding of our own civilization than it has confused the interpretations of archaeologists dealing with the dead past. . . . Secularism is not essentially a product of the city. There are

[16] *Op. cit.*
[17] F. Boulard and J. Remy, *Pratique Religieuse Urbaine et Régions Culturelles* (Paris, 1968).
[18] E. Evans-Pritchard, *Nuer Religion* (Oxford, 1956), p. 311.

secular tribal cultures. Until he grasps this fact, the anthropologist himself is at a loss to interpret his own material. When he comes across an irreligious tribe, he redoubles the vigour and subtlety of his inquiries. He tries to squeeze his information harder to make it yield that overall superstructure of symbolism which his analysis can relate all through the book to the social substructure, or he dredges for at very least something to put in a final chapter on religion."[19]

Thus, some primitive societies have complex religious systems, as in the case of the Nuer. Some are strict in their devotions, others casual or sceptical. The relevant variable is not the degree of industrialization, and generalizations cannot be made on this assumption.

III. INDICES OF RELIGIOSITY

The third crucial assumption upon which the secularization debate rests relates to definitions of religion itself. The nature of religious experience is peculiarly difficult to define. What is piety to one man is superstition to another. What is essential to some is peripheral to others. Simple enough: but for many years those aspects of religious behaviour which have been selected for investigation have been of an immediately observable kind. Just as legalism dies hard amongst theologians, so too does positivism amongst sociologists.

If religion or religious experience is accepted as being nothing more than formal church affiliation or participation and the like, then sociologists like Bryan Wilson are plainly in the right when they describe the decline of religion in societies like Britain and the United States.[20] The statistics which are available do indeed show that church attendance is declining, that the numbers of religious personnel are declining and their status is marginal in society, that the churches are limiting their claims for various areas of life, and so on. But if religious experience is seen as being something more than the straight counts that the positivist tradition in sociology and the legalistic tradition in the churches would have it, then there are a good many more methodological problems with which we have to deal.

[19] Mary Douglas, *Natural Symbols* (London, 1970), p. x.
[20] B. Wilson, *Religion in Secular Society* (London, 1966).

David Martin, who has also spoken of the impossibility of separating the religious and the secular sphere, writes of the concept of secularization as: "a tool of counter-religious ideologies which identify the 'real' element in religion for polemical purposes and then arbitrarily relate it to the notion of a unitary and irreversible process, partly for the aesthetic satisfactions found in such notions and partly as a psychological boost to the movements with which they are associated".[21]

Is it possible in those societies where church attendance is no longer a part of expected behaviour to seek for indices of religious experience which go beyond the narrower confines of participation in organized religious rituals?

In his book, *The Invisible Religion*, the German sociologist Thomas Luckmann deals very cogently with the problems of locating religion in industrialized societies. In his criticisms of the currently impoverished state of the sociology of religion, he focuses on the identification of "church" with "religion" and the consequent narrowing of vision: "In the absence of a well-founded theory, secularization is typically regarded as a process of religious pathology to be measured by the shrinking reach of the churches. Since the institutional vacuum is not being filled by a counter-church—which was still envisaged by Comte—one readily concludes that modern society is non-religious. It matters little that the process is evaluated negatively by those sociologists of religion who have inner or professional commitments to the churches; their model of interpretation is borrowed from the positivistic thesis. The churches remain, in a manner of speaking, islands of religion (or irrationality) in a sea of secularism (or reason). It only remains for the sociologist of religion to analyse the national and class differences in the process of religious decline—that is, of the shrinking reach of the churches."[22]

Luckmann argues that seeking to explain the changes in one institution by changes in another is sociologically naïve; he suggests that by seeing the relationship between industrialization and secularization as indirect a different perspective is possible: "Industrialization and urbanization were processes that rein-

[21] David Martin, *The Religious and the Secular* (London, 1969), pp. 16–17.
[22] *Op. cit.*, p. 23.

forced the tendency of institutional specialization. Institutional specialization, in turn, tended to 'free' the norms of all the various institutional areas from the influence of the originally superordinated 'religious' values...the reality of the religious cosmos waned in proportion to its shrinking social base; to wit, specialized religious institutions. What were originally total life values became part-time norms. In short, the decrease in traditional church religion may be seen as a consequence of the shrinking relevance of the values, institutionalized in church religion, for the integration and legitimation of everyday life in modern society."[23]

His book is concerned with working out a new perspective for interpreting religion in those forms which are not immediately visible is theoretically possible.

Geertz's general comments on the anthropologist's methodological problems of locating religion in society are relevant here. He points out that it is difficult "to get phenomenologically accurate descriptions of religious experience",[24] since investigating what religion means to people usually has to be undertaken after instead of during their involvement in worship. For him the symbols and images of a faith are crucial as means of understanding. "What sacred symbols do for those to whom they are sacred is to formulate an image of the world's construction and a programme for human conduct that are mere reflexes of one another."[25] Difficult though it is, the empirical task is to describe "the way in which religious belief appears to the believer".[26]

It is precisely this dimension which has so far been largely lacking in sociological analyses. Little attempt has been made to discover what is regarded as religion by the believer, not by the outsider. That the location and analysis of the less immediately visible aspects of religious behaviour and thinking is empirically an exceptionally difficult task is undoubtedly true, involving as it does long-term immersion in the lives of the communities studied rather than fleeting trips. It is much easier to concentrate on discovering the socio-economic components of church congregations than to discover the religious perspectives of a general population.

[23] *Op. cit.*, p. 39.
[25] *Op. cit.*, p. 97.
[24] *Op. cit.*, p. 108.
[26] *Op. cit.*, p. 99.

But it would be false to think of this as being a problem unique to the sociology of religion. In all areas of sociological interest there is a temptation to rely upon the positivist tradition and to stick to the more readily recognizable indices of social reality. Thus, the findings of kinship studies in the United States and Britain, with their concentration upon items such as the frequency of family interaction, frequently fail to discuss the qualitative aspects of family relationships and the effects these have upon individual behaviour. The reader coming fresh to them might indeed wonder if their authors lived in the same societies as those described from other perspectives—by Eugene O'Neill, say, or R. D. Laing.

What is needed now is not so much new theoretical formulations for studying religion in industrial societies, since these are already available, in embryonic form at least, but rather the long-term study of the religious orientations of members of industrialized societies, seen from *their* perspectives, not those which have already been presupposed to exist. This would not only give us a more imaginative sociology; it might also add to our understanding of the nature of religion itself.

William and Nancy McCready

Socialization and the Persistence of Religion

I. Introduction

TRADITIONAL practitioners of the sociology of religion have focused on devotional behaviour and church membership as the "effects" of religious commitment. A discussion of the persistence of "the religious" in modern society typically begins with a mass of data "proving" that devotion and membership are on the wane and therefore religion is disappearing. On the contrary, religion is complex behaviour and religious behaviour is not an end in itself, but rather a symbol of the person's understanding of the world around him. Another type of complex behaviour that exposes an understanding of the world is the way in which persons define and conceive of their sex roles, masculine and feminine. These conceptions of reality, the "religious" and the "sexual", are acquired in, and influenced by, the socialization process. As people grow to adulthood they learn "religious" and "sexual" interpretive methods for making sense out of the conditions surrounding them. The persistence of religion is intimately tied to this double process of "religious" and "sex role" socialization.

The respected American anthropologist Clifford Geertz has proposed the following working definition of "religion": "Religion is a system of symbols which acts to establish powerful, persuasive and long-lasting moods and motivations in men by formulating conceptions of a general order of existence, and clothing these conceptions with such an aura of factuality that the moods and motivations seem uniquely realistic."[1]

[1] C. Geertz, "Religion as a Cultural System", in *Religious Situation 1968* (Boston, 1968), pp. 639–87.

This is a much broader conception of the "religious" than definitions which utilize devotional behaviour or church membership. Geertz focuses on the way in which the individual perceives the world in which he lives. Religion is concerned with "a general order of existence", and is therefore transcendental in nature. This definition of religion lays bare the ultimate question of life: Is the Really Real fundamentally good or bad, benevolent or malign?

Any human conception about the general order of existence is a "meaning system", that is to say it is the template an individual uses to interpret what happens to him. Ordinarily the "common sense" meaning system is sufficient to explain the circumstances. However, every so often something happens that does not respond to a common sense analysis. A tragedy or ecstasy that is outside of the usual experience in life needs to be integrated and explained by the individual.

Man does not come into the world with a ready-made religious meaning system, it is developed through the process of socialization. The individual must learn who and what he is, and how to make sense out of his surroundings. "Socialization" is a learning phenomenon that takes place in the family first, then later in other less personal institutions. The end result of this process is the creation of a meaning system within the individual, which he then uses to interpret "the general order of existence".

Sex role identification is also developed through socialization. Such identification is the set of symbols that the individual uses to locate himself or herself in the relative social positions of "male" and "female". A minimum definition of male and female is provided by the human biological system, but the personal definitions of masculine and feminine are more complicated learned behaviours. Our thesis is that religious socialization and sex role socialization are intimately connected activities, and that as long as one exists so will the other. Therefore religious behaviour will persist through the processes of the evolution of meaning systems.

II. SEX ROLE SOCIALIZATION

"Sex role" means the constellation of qualities a person understands to characterize males and females in his culture. Socialization research has produced information that can be summarized in the following three points. First of all, sex role definition occurs at an early age within the family as part of the intimate relationships between parents and their children, therefore it has a primordial quality. Secondly, this type of role definition occurs primarily between a father and his children. And thirdly, there are important differences between boys and girls as to the ultimate effects of this socialization process.

All of the literature describing human socialization points to the fact that it occurs within the family. The composition of the unit may vary from culture to culture, but the importance of this locus is undeniable. The young child first sees "males" and "females" as behaviourally differentiated models to be imitated within the family. A common assumption has always been that boys learned how to be men by watching their fathers, and that girls learned how to be women by watching their mothers. This is only partially true. Recent research into the development of sex roles has shed added light on the relative importance of fathers and mothers in the process. The American psychologist Jean Block has come to the following conclusion: "Apart from the substantive socialization issues, the data from this study suggest that the father appears to be a far more crucial agent in directing and channelling the sex-typing of the child, both male and female, than has been supposed."[2] Block bases this on the observation that fathers emphasize self-initiative in their sons and the development of close, interpersonal relationships in their daughters more than mothers.

Block uses the dichotomous conception of the modality of all living forms developed by David Bakan to describe the process of sex role socialization.[3] Bakan identifies two modes of existence, "agency" and "communion". Agency is concerned with the organism as an individual and manifests itself in self-protection, self-assertion and self-expansion. Communion describes the organism as it exists in some larger organism and manifests itself in

[2] Jean H. Block, *Conceptions of Sex Role: Some Cross-cultural and Longitudinal Perspectives*, paper presented at the Bernard Moses Lecture at the Institute of Human Development at the University of California (Berkeley, 1971), p. 12.
[3] D. Bakan, *The Duality of Human Existence* (Chicago, 1966).

the sense of being at one with the other organism. According to Bakan human development is the blending of these two modes of existence, the tempering of agency with communion. In a discussion of sex role socialization this translates into the tempering of the masculine (agency) with the feminine (communion) to produce androgynous individuals who can display and utilize both their agentic and communal talents. The following typology categorizes the models stemming from possible parental combinations.

Mother

		Communal	Agentic
F a t h e r	Communal	A	B
	Agentic	C	D

A. No role model of agency for the children.
B. Androgynous model for the children.
C. Traditional sex role model for the children.
D. No role model of communion for the children.

Men and women who make up the type "B" category depict a parental pair in which neither mother nor father exemplify the typical cultural sex-role stereotypes, but rather where both parents are salient and provide models for their children of competence, tolerance, consideration of others, and a sharing, rather segmenting of responsibilities. Unrestrained agency leads to exploitation and unproductive egocentricism, while unchecked communion leads to passivity and a lack of initiative in the individual. Maturity requires a blending of these two modes of living.

The third point of interest in the socialization process is the fact that there are differences in the process for males and females. Block's research shows that there is an emphasis on the development of agency for little boys and on the development of communion for little girls. Therefore for men, self-assertion, self-interest and self-extension need to be tempered by considerations of mutuality, interdependence and joint-welfare. For women the submersion of self, the concern for a harmonious functioning of the group, and the importance of a consensus should be amended to include the agentic aspects of living: self-assertion and self-actualization.

Inspection of Block's data reveals that different issues arise between fathers and sons, and mothers and daughters. Father-son issues centre around question of authority and mother-daughter issues focus on the mother's struggle to maintain her own autonomy. Further analysis reveals that the father-child issues, for both sons and daughters, are more important to the children than are mother-child issues.

Sex role socialization provides a meaning system which includes symbols about "the way things really are", but it does not necessarily include any explicit transcendental conception of reality. Children learn about the world and what is expected of them sexually. They learn the "appropriate" responses for men and women engaged in primary group behaviour. They learn the nature of The Sexual from the atmosphere created by the relationship between their parents. The process of religious socialization has many similarities to the process of sex role development, but shifts the emphasis to an explicitly transcendental conception of reality.

III. Religious Socialization

Recent research by one of the authors, W. McCready, into the process of religious socialization has revealed three points that are salient to the present discussion and similar to the findings about sex role socialization.[4] First, "religiousness" is something that develops within the family through the influence of the parents on their children. Secondly, it is transmitted primarily between fathers and their children. Thirdly, there are important differences between the boys' and girls' processes in terms of the influence of the quality of the parental relationship.

These data reveal the pre-eminence of the parents' influence on the devotional behaviour of their children, both boys and girls. The following path diagrams show the relative strengths of these influences.[5]

[4] W. McCready, *Faith of Our Fathers*, unpublished Ph.D. dissertation in the Dept. of Sociology at the University of Illinois at Chicago Circle, 1972.
[5] The decimal numbers are path coefficients derived from a multiple regression equation and they indicate the strength of the relationship between the two variables accounting for all of the other variables in the model. For a complete explanation see Otis D. Duncan, "Path Analysis: Sociological Examples", *American Journal of Sociology*, vol. 72 (July, 1966), pp. 1–16.

Fig. 1. *Boy's Public Devotion*

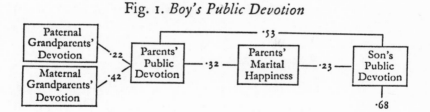

Fig. 2. *Girl's Public Devotion*

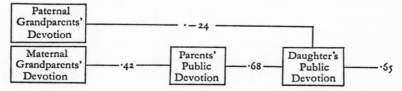

Note that the parents are the dominant influence in both diagrams (having greater impact than such traditionally favoured factors as social class and the denomination of schooling).[6] In every instance when the influence of the parents was separated into the contribution of the father and the mother, fathers had more influence on their children than mothers did. Thus there is empirical confirmation for points one and two.

The most interesting finding, for our present discussion, is the way in which "parents' marital happiness" influences the devotional behaviour of the children. This factor has a clear impact on the son's devotional behaviour and no discernible impact on the daughter's devotion. In other words, sons are sensitive to the relationship between their parents in a way that daughters are not. Why should this be so? The son is in a triadic relationship with his father and mother. He relates to his father as an authority and to his mother as an object of his affection. The daughter, on the other hand, is in a basically dyadic relationship with her father who is both an authority and an object of her affection. Therefore the son is likely to be more sensitive to tension between his parents because he has to "manage" relationships to both of them. The daughter is not that intimately tied

[6] Social class and the denomination of the high school for both parents and children were originally in the equation but have been removed from this presentation because of their extremely low influence and the requirements of space.

to her mother and can afford to observe a little marital tension once in a while.

IV. The Evolution of a Meaning System

Interpretations of reality, symbolized by devotional behaviour, are transmitted from one generation to the next. Devotion has long been considered an indicator of religious involvement by sociologists, but it has ordinarily been interpreted as a substitute for more "mature" human activity. As Dr Brothers points out, in another article in this issue, "religious" has come to be equated with "primitive", and "secular" has come to mean "modern". This equation can be extended further by noting that "religious-primitive" has come to mean "unreal-false" while "secular-modern" has come to mean "real-true". Some social scientists currently consider the primitive and primordial in man to be dangerous to social progress, while the secular and empirical are thought to be instrumental towards that end. This viewpoint ignores the symbolic nature of human behaviour and ignores the factor of the transcendent in human activity. The things men do expose their understanding of the nature of the Real, and this fact ought to be taken into account by social scientists in their analysis. Good social science can attempt to "get inside" of the symbol of "devotion" and find out what it means to the devout person, rather than to the detached observer. Symbols of ultimate meaning are never easy to uncover and even more difficult to understand. Mircea Eliade addressed himself to this problem a decade ago: "An essential characteristic of religious symbolism is its multivalence, its capacity to express simultaneously several meanings the unity between which is not evident on the plane of immediate experience. . . . This capacity has an important consequence: the symbol is capable of revealing a perspective in which diverse realities can be fitted together or even integrated into a 'system'."[7]

Both "sexual" and "religious" symbols are multivalent, to use Eliade's term. A narrowly defined sex role, either male or female, is a severe limitation on the individual's personality. The very "narrowness" of the self-definition means several different things.

[7] Mircea Eliade, *The Two and the One* (New York, 1962), p. 203.

If a person sees himself as living within narrow constraints and bound by harsh social sanctions, his image of "God" will be concomitantly severe. A narrow sexual role reveals a person's narrow meaning system. Sexual role playing reflects a person's thinking about the way "things ought to be", and as such it is moral and religious behaviour. If a person defies the sexual role that is appropriate for him, he can expect the "really Real", or whatever conception of an ultimate personal power he may have, to judge him harshly for having stepped outside the bounds of acceptable social behaviour.

The previously demonstrated connection between devotional behaviour and primordial factors, such as happiness and sex role, indicates that the "sexual" and "religious" socialization processes are totally interdependent. The way individuals define their own reality consists of both sexual and religious symbolism. Human beings develop a personal relation to an ultimate power which they sexualize, and a conception of the nature of the Real which, in the Geertzian schema, is "religious". Both of these "meaning systems" evolve within the socialization process.

A person can grow up narrow or expansive, judgmental or explorative, agentic or communal, or he can develop combinations of these attributes, depending on his or her socialization experience. The relationship between "sexual" and "religious" socialization is a fact of life and it determines the individual's level of maturity. The expansiveness of the "religious" conception of the Real, that is whether it is viewed as benevolent or malign, is constrained by the "sexual" definition of the self as male or female. If the sex role is rigid and narrow, then the "religious reality" will be limited to the agentic for men and the communal for women. Tenderness and co-operation will not fit within the male's definition of the "possible world", and self-initiative will be outside the realm of possibility for the women.

On the other hand, if the sex role is expansive and the nature of the Real is benevolent the potential maturity of the individual is unlimited. Ignoring the relationship between sex role development and the religious meaning system producs immaturity. Individuals grow to adulthood repeating the same sexual and religious conflicts over and over again, never resolving anything. It is possible to ignore the relationship between "sexual" and "religious" socialization but the price is high. The mature person requires an androgynous blend of agency and communion in both the sexual and religious elements of his meaning system if he is to fulfil his potential for growth.

V. ANDROGYNOUS SOCIALIZATION

The person comes to a sense of himself or herself before he or she learns to walk or forms words. Children begin to develop a meaning system based on their own self-concepts. They do this through their parents, who are interpreters of reality, language and meaning to them. How a boy or girl ultimately approaches the universe is irrevocably bonded to their conception of their own reality.

As previously stated, this is simultaneously a religious and a sexual process. Sexuality is the most pervasive and visible characteristic of the human being from birth to death. All other development occurs within the context of sexuality. The resolution of primary sexual conflicts determines whether the individual achieves maturity or whether he remains fixated at an infantile level.

In order for a person to develop the most mature faith (i.e., surrender to what one knows as the highest worth for man) his sexual self-concept must be one of expansion, wholeness and a unity of agency and communion. The person of great religious development is one who has become androgenous in his conception of his own sexuality.

In loving intercourse a man and woman are conscious of both ecstasy and sorrow. Lovers are ecstatic in their physical union, in their oneness beyond any other experience between human beings. They are also aware of an aloneness, a highly physical separateness from the beloved. They must fall back from each other as two persons who can come together only temporarily in that union of flesh. Love-making is a highly expressive symbol because it exposes the reaching of man to become one, and, in that human act, the ultimate conclusion of remaining two.

The German romantic Franz von Baader has written that human love-making is, ". . . to help man and woman to integrate internally the complete human image, that is to say the divine and original image".[8] Eliade interprets this as an exhortation to create an androgynous image, blending the masculine and feminine in the intercourse symbol, but not necessarily in fact.[9] In other words the symbol may be used by the unmarried and celibate as well as the married.

Christianity has evidence of exactly this kind of interpretation and of reconciling the opposites in our experience. St Paul and the Gospel of St John speak of androgyny as a characteristic of spiritual perfection. Jesus is described as saying that the kingdom would come when "the two shall be one, the outside like the inside, the male with the female neither male nor female".[10]

What is the effect of androgynous parents on their children? This is the logical question to be raised in light of the relationship between socialization and the persistence of the religious. The parental model of androgyny stands in direct contrast to the typical socialization model in which communion is stressed for girls and agency is stressed for boys. Girls are taught to seek their fulfilment exclusively through the creation of a family and boys are expected to find complete happiness in the successes of the world of work. The androgynous parental model stresses the complimentary qualities in the individual children.

The father who has developed his capacity for tenderness, expression and co-operation will be a witness to his son that "maleness" is more than aggression and domination and that it is good for him to develop the expansive side of his personality. This father will also be a witness to his daughter that she can legitimately expect and even demand an expanded image of "maleness" from the men she deals with.

The mother who combines agency and communion and has developed her capacity for self-direction and self-assertion will be a witness to her daughter that initiative and firmness of mind are desirable attributes in a woman. She will also be a witness to her son that such women are pleasant to deal with and make attractive partners with whom to share the adventure of living.

How one sees the rest of reality is bound up with this pro-

[8] E. Susini, *Franz von Baader et le romantisme mystique* (Paris, 1942).
[9] M. Eliade, *op. cit*, p. 102.
[10] Second epistle of Clement, quoted in J. Doresse, *Les livres secrets de gnostiques d'Egypt* (Paris, 1958).

cess and is the basis for how one views God. A joke currently being circulated in the United States has a young ghetto black reading the Bible. His teacher asks if he has learned anything. "Yes," says the young man, "all about this 'God cat'." His teacher says, "Well that's very good, what's he like?" The student retorts with, "She's black, man."

The Divine is neither male nor female, but both. It is interesting that the words of the creation, "let us make them in our image, male and female", have customarily been interpreted to signify the division of the race into two opposed segments. It makes more sense to interpret these words to mean that both male and female are combined in every individual and that that is the image of the Divine.

The search for the transcendent, for that which cannot be explained by our experience, the search for God, is a search for unity, for a way to make sense out of all the fragments and apparent contradictions of our experiences. The androgynous self can come nearer the resemblance of that oneness, the imaginative and powerful wholeness which is beyond ourselves, and begin to be a witness to that reality.

How can anyone be a child of God, entrust and surrender to an almighty Being, if that Being is not first a nurturing being, a mothering, feminine power? How can a person become an adult with a mature faith without a God with whom he may join in the work of redemption, a God with whom he may share the initiative and aggression of spreading the fierce and gentle tale of the Word, the good news.

God is a mother, a father, a brother, a sister, a friend and a lover. He has said to us that we must become like Him, perfect. How can we seek to become this whole, this one, unless we too develop a wholeness of that which threatens to most severely separate us, men from women? The development of the "masculine" in women and the "feminine" in men as individual reflections of the Divine is the most mature opportunity open to man. The androgynous meaning system, evolved through the processes of sexual and religious socialization, is a new synthesis which can fertilize the religious dimension of man's existence in the future. As long as boys grow into men and girls into women, "the religious" will persist in human life.

Jean Remy and Emile Servais

The Functions of the Occult and the Mysterious in Contemporary Society

IN ORDER to say what are the functions of the occult in contemporary society, we must first try to define the social meaning of the phenomena normally covered by this term. Normal usage calls "occult" illegitimate social practices which must remain hidden in order to exist. In other words, the first stage of the analysis will place the occult in the sociological category of illegitimate practices, and in the particular sector of that category where the illegitimate combines with the sacred. This will allow us to make a connection and a distinction between the occult and the mysterious. The combination of these two dimensions defines the phenomena with which we shall be dealing and places our analysis of magical phenomena within the religious field. This twofold dimension will make it possible to explain a relation to the world and show, in a second stage, how contemporary society induces it and does so unequally as between different social groups.

I. ILLEGITIMATE FORMS OF THE OCCULT AND THE SACRED

By combining the categories of the sacred and the legitimate or illegitimate, we hope to show the socially produced character of the phenomena which normal usage defines as occult and mysterious.

1. *The Legitimate and the Sacred*
Legitimacy is what gives a social order validity. It is a quality

attributed to a system of norms by virtue of which the system is accepted and recognized as having authority. Within this framework, every social action is internally motivated and can therefore be described as "moral". This idea implies a system of principles which derive their force from an apparent naturalness, while in fact they are the result of a social construction. These principles are arbitrary, though not perceived as such, and determine the way in which society selects the realities which deserve to be the objects of thought and action, and their order of priority. This implies cultural conditions which are the source of the spontaneous credibility attributed to certain acts.

On the other hand, ambivalence seems to us characteristic of the sacred dimension which is attributed to social realities. This dimension can be seen as soon as a person or a group develops an attitude made up of both attraction and repulsion. This ambivalence is the basis of the perception of the mysterious. From that point the sacred universe appears as the universe which dominates us and which cannot be mastered from within. The ambivalent attitude developed by the sacred originates in the process of symbolization in which signifiers, everyday objects and actions, are regarded as revealing objects of a different order.

To the extent to which the group or person takes up an asymmetrical relation, that is, one of dependence or respect, to these realities created by the process of symbolization, the ambivalence becomes the stronger and the sacred dimension takes on its full significance in the same way as the apprehension of the mysterious. From one point of view the sacred object is that which tends to impose itself as a totality. On the one hand it becomes the focal point around which the person structures himself, while on the other it expresses the values around which the unity of the group is formed. It is characterized by its capacity to create collective mobilization out of affective mobilization. The type of relation adopted by the group towards the sacred object depends on the one hand on the particular characteristics of its sacredness, whether it is personal or impersonal, and on the other hand on an attitude of abandonment without calculation or calculated exploitation.

This type of perception is distributed in function of the social conditions of a given group and of the general state of society as a whole. For our purposes we shall combine the dimension of the sacred with that of the legitimate, although the sacred may be on either side of the border between the legitimate and the illegitimate. The attitude towards the sacred which is defined as legitimate is determined by the social group dominant in a society, that is the group which has succeeded in giving its aims priority in the society.

2. Religion and the Social Construction of the Perception of the Legitimate Sacred

The legitimate dimension of the sacred is based on the development of autonomy in the religious sphere. This autonomy is normally produced by the formation of a group of specialists capable of defining the sphere and guaranteeing the legitimate attitude towards the sacred.

This body of specialists gains influence easily because its function is first of all to provide affective security in relations with the sphere of the sacred experienced as the important sphere, that is, as a crucial sphere in the constitution of legitimate order. This affective security implies ritualization, formal mastery of gestures with the assurance that they are being performed correctly.

Being the antithesis of this, the illegitimate sacred will assert itself in turn by various types of inversion, either of ritual or even of the conception of the sacred, which will most probably be seen more in impersonal terms and in a relation of manipulation and calculation, its function often being to make up by roundabout means for a lack of power. The illegitimate sacred can be discovered *a contrario* from the legitimate sacred. In certain cases, even, it is reduced to an inverse appropriation of legitimate symbolism. In this case it is probably the only way in which groups deprived of the social capacity to produce and promote their own symbols can give themselves a measure of autonomy.

Independently of the intentional or non-intentional character of this opposition, it is always seen as a profanation by the dominant group. This type of perception emphasizes the social importance of the sacred and its affective character. It is regarded as an extremely important area both for individual and for social order. This importance is increased by the way in which the sacred moves between the two, and is expressed and revealed by its affective impact. The social importance of the sacred is the result of its carrying a powerful charge of legitimacy, whether positive, supporting the established order, or negative, supporting a rejection of that order.

To the extent to which the areas regarded as occult are associated with a perception of the mysterious, they also possess some of the ambivalence of the sacred and are the object of strong disapproval mixed with respect and fear. It is also possible for them to enjoy semi-legitimacy and an attraction which constitute the full ambiguity of negative sacredness (the categories of the demonic). In this connection it would be interesting to analyse the myth of the Jew in European history, which appears in association with the occult, the mysterious and commerce with demons.

On the basis of these sociological remarks about the dimensions of the sacred and the legitimate we can reinterpret the attribution, in common usage, of the terms "occult" and "mysterious" to certain social phenomena. Any social manifestation connected with the illegitimate order cannot find full public social expression. Such expression is only possible if those who engage in such practices regard them as valid in spite of the disapproval of the dominant group. It may even be thought that the performers of such practices will accept this disapproval all the more easily, even if they have to keep their actions secret, if they regard the practices as valid while they are rejected by religion and society.

We would therefore maintain with some confidence that practices which common usage describes as "occult" are such only because they are socially illegitimate, because they are defined as occult by the dominant religious or social group.

II. THE CONDITIONS FOR THE APPEARANCE OF THE SACRED

Our analysis of the legitimate or illegitimate sacred needs to be deepened by an investigation of the conditions under which the sacred appears. We shall consider in particular socio-economic conditions on the one hand and the degree of legitimacy accorded to religion on the other.

Within the same system different social groups have different positions as a result of their differing degree of mastery of socio-economic and technical codes. Their possible relations to the sacred depend both on these conditions and on the strength or weakness of religion.

1. *Socio-Economic Conditions*

A social group which is characterized by insecurity of employment and therefore by irregularity of income will tend to see life as a gamble, since all its experience is the result not of a choice but of factors which it cannot control. If it is then made to attribute responsibility for its situation to an evil, hidden God and personal and impersonal powers, it will try to conciliate them indirectly. Its conditions of life have given it a vision of the world based on specific difficulties caused by specific persons, and the unifying factor of this vision tends to be feeling. Members of this group appropriate what dominates them, or tend to do so, through the mode of resignation, or indirectly through "personalized" intermediaries or "contacts", from which they expect no more than a vague result since everything is in the end a matter of luck, including the choice of a good "contact".

Poor and unstable socio-economic conditions tend to produce a sacral vision of a world over which one can gain control either through intermediaries capable of bringing immediate relief, happiness here and now, or through dreams. In the second case, though, there is a clean break with reality because the aspirations which fill the dreams bear no relation to objective possibilities. The useful intermediary is the one who can tell you how to win the pools and how to solve all your problems by a miraculous windfall or at any rate without effort. It is possible that small farmers or small shopkeepers today form one of the groups which are particularly liable to have such a vision of the world and their relation to the world as creates a need for personalized intermediaries who can tell you straightway if you ought to sell up and get out or whether there's still a chance.[1]

On the other hand, people whose economic prospects are more secure tend to develop a view of the world in which control through real action is central. What is then sacralized is not so

---

[1] Claude Fischler, "Astrologie et Société", in *Le retour des astrologues*, Dossier du *Nouvel Observateur* (1971), p. 72.

much the world itself as the order which prevails in the world
and the necessity to conform to technical or moral rules in order
to acquire control of it. Economic security may, however, also
produce a view which regards the world essentially as a game.
In contrast to the previous situation, there is no longer a confusion between the game and reality. Social life may be lived by
two codes which do not influence each other, not only in the
serious mode but also in the mode of the non-serious, the
gratuitous and the useless. In this case recourse to socially illegitimate practices does not destructure those who perform them
and does not prevent their having an effective strategy. It is probably such groups which develop a critical attitude towards explicit symbolism. What in this case becomes the symbolic and
the legitimate sacred is a "personal" construction of significant
relations independent of explicit social guarantees.

Socio-economic conditions therefore produce practices which
are called illegitimate by groups which judge them or which are
capable of making their attitude dominant. The incorrect use
of technical or ethical codes, or their use in an unserious mode,
for example, will be declared illegitimate by the group whose
vision of the world is organized around seriousness and order.

2. Strong or Weak Legitimacy of Religion

In a society dominated by positivism, that is, in which anything which wishes to be believed must be presented as the result
of empirical verification, religion may come to be assimilated to
illegitimate practices. The symbolic link between the individual
and what transcends him is expressed by practices which are
illegitimate or enjoy weak legitimacy because they cannot be empirically verified. In the case in which religious language is in an
inferior position to scientific language, official religious practices
enjoy only semi-legitimacy. In other societies the position is re-
versed, and it is then religion which determines the perception
of the legitimate sacred. So, for example, in the seventeenth century astrology was relegated to the category of the occult by
Catholicism and rationalism. It was at the end of the seventeenth
century that the combination of the Catholic counter-offensive
against heresies and the remains of paganism and the rationalist
scientific offensive against magic relegated astrology into the

ghetto of the occult. The astrology which had already ceased to be a religion was henceforth no longer a science. It was denounced as superstition, and rightly, because "with the secession of astronomy astrology no longer took part in the work and research of the laboratory."[2]

The practice of communication with spirits is another example which illustrates the degree of legitimacy of religion. Such practices are generally only described as legitimate to the extent that they are controlled by the religious institution. Control over spirits by means of exorcisms in certain religious rites enjoyed high legitimacy only a short time ago, which was not true of control over spirits through mediums.

Max Weber showed how religion which enjoys a high degree of legitimacy can give social status to a magical consultation by transforming it into the cure of souls.[3] In any case the one is very close to the other in that in both cases the relation and the distribution of "graces" is individualized.

Fundamentally a practice based on a client relationship receives legitimacy through ethical systematization. This reappropriation is based on the inability of priests to control the charism of prophecy while still needing to exercise practical influence on the conduct of laymen. The last parts of our analysis reveal certain structural conditions and do not concern the meaning experienced and transmitted by the participants.

III. Modernity and the Legitimate or Illegitimate Sacred

We would describe modernity as the situation which confers legitimacy on scientific and technical procedures, on the sense of calculation and productivity which reduces everything to needs to be satisfied by a calculated effort, and on the creation of a particular universe which gives a high value to control of the world on the basis of the right to privacy and individual autonomy. In so far as explicit symbols appear as the universe still beyond man's control, modernity has among other consequences the erosion of symbols which are part or coherent totalizing systems. The situation may then arise in which the occult and

---

[2] E. Morin, *Le retour des astrologues, op. cit.,* p. 116.
[3] M. Weber, *Economie et Société* (Paris, 1971), p. 487.

the mysterious now develop as a phenomenon involving not marginal groups but the middle class, and in which the "modern" sacred in its "illegitimate" manifestations presents itself in the characteristics of the counter-image of modernity. In this case it will contribute in a different way to the increasing marginalization of religion.

1. *Control by Means of Science and Calculation*

The development of science and technology has given society the means to achieve, in a controlled way, a set of goals of its own choice. The new ability to forecast combines with an emphasis on a productive rationality whose main aim is exploitation through calculation to produce the idea of a game without mystery and of efficient organizations which make no demand on the emotions. This control tends to claim that any problem is soluble through knowledge or conformity to certain rules. Even the future becomes subject to control, and our predictions help us to choose one of the several possible types of society. Such claims are the expression of a universe of legitimacy which gives rise to heavily valued social practices, but they too do not necessarily correspond to a description of the objective possibilities.

This scientific world also develops very elaborate codes. These are on the one hand quite commonplace, in that they can be appropriated by anyone capable of the necessary effort, and on the other hand, being highly elaborate, cannot spread easily. This gives a monopoly to the group of scientists which is alone capable of judging the quality of its work.

Because of this, the science capable of giving power and control is perceived as the monopoly of a special category which becomes the world of the scientist and outside of which there comes into being the category of the profane, that is, of those who are not and cannot be initiated. This scientific universe sometimes becomes the basis for stories which have all the characteristics of mythical tales. This is the case, for example, with spy stories in which a scientific formula capable of giving power to the political group which possesses it is sought by all sides and finally stolen by a group of outsiders who are not even sure of having stolen the right formula and must depend again on the scientist to decode it. The scientist in this case may be someone rejected by the scientific community. Here again we have the monopoly and the inversions which formerly characterized the relations between the priest, the layman and the sacrilegious in the world of religion. We can thus see how the characteristics of the sacred world now subtly and secretly infiltrate a universe which gives a high value to control. It is interesting to note that this reappropriation may be given public expression because it is at the heart of current social legitimacy. In a universe in which legitimacy was dominated by religion, such an attribution of the characteristics of the sacred to science would have been socially repressed and could only have been expressed in the world of the occult.

Pursuing this approach, we could examine science fiction, in which science has at the same time the power to terrify and the power to fascinate. The basis of this universe in which science belongs to the order of the fascinating and the mysterious is the fact that scientific and technological power is not accessible equally to all.

2. Control over an Individual Universe: Individualization and the Right to Privacy

Modernity is equally the basis of the legitimacy and status given to the private sphere, the area within the control of the individual and his interpersonal relations.

This universe within his own control gives the individual, at least on the level of his perceptions, the possibility of creating his own meanings, organized around a right to individualized happiness and the will to seek it methodically. Once again there is a reappropriation of the rationality of control and exploitation. The result is an ambiguity, because this aim carries on the one hand the potential of individual development and on the other the potential of isolation and loneliness. This ambiguity is expressed all the more as distance enters contacts themselves. While society multiplies the possibilities of contact between individuals, the individuals themselves may appear to each other as increasingly distant and foreign. This appears very sharply if we contrast the norms of traditional society, in which the basic relations of social life were primary relations which organized encounters with others around a personal and affective dimension. These models of traditional society in which interpersonal relations were the basis of social regulation continue to operate, but find their main expression in the private world. The private world only makes sense in opposition to the public world, which appears in many respects as a world in which important things happen but which is controlled by impersonal self-regulating mechanisms. This creates an opposition between the world valued by the person as the scene of his creativity and the world of important events, which is dominated by collective control and may be perceived as an anonymous machine.

When the interpersonal continues to be the familiar world, but restricted to the private sphere, the public sphere with which dealings are inevitable is perceived as beyond personal control, and in extreme cases as a magma of anonymous forces which must be conciliated as the primitive tries to conciliate nature. This is the picture of the anonymous city, the mysterious underground network which is the scene of some detective stories, where the fear of being liquidated, of being seen, can only be overcome through the mediation of the hero who knows the intricacies and the laws of this world and is thus capable of helping its victims.

This collective world beyond individual control may easily appear as an illegitimate world because it does not conform to the rule of perfect transparency, which is a basic element in the picture of a truly democratic society, another aspect of contemporary legitimacy which we have not analysed here.[4] So the detective story frequently invokes a system of occult forces. In this respect it is interesting to compare the occult character which results from lack of control with the world surrounding the myth of the scientist in which the occult is not invoked. In the scientific myth the occult is only invoked when there is an illegitimate use of science, when it is not used in the service of a world of individualized happiness but to secure the success of some opposed aim (the use of science for terrorism both in fictional worlds and in the world of social practice).

[4] This aspect has been discussed by Jean Remy in "Opinion publique, groupe de pression et autorité constituée. Contribution à une théorie de la légitimité religieuse", *Social Compass*, 2 (1972).

3. The Middle Class and Cultural Insecurity

Insecurity normally gives rise to reassuring practices, which have been mentioned previously in connection with ritualization. Reassuring practices may be either legitimate or illegitimate, and a distinction has been made between popular religion and religion affecting anarchic groups which is based on a ritualization in part at least illegitimate. The strength of these practices often forces religious leaders to reappropriate them and grant them semi-legitimacy. The phenomenon we wish to describe is one of ritualization by means of practices which differ from popular religion on two points. On the one hand, it affects the middle classes not as a result of economic insecurity but as a result of cultural insecurity, and on the other it cannot be defined in relation to official religion, which feels neither profaned nor obliged to reappropriate it.

The middle class can be defined by a double negation, first of that which it no longer is and which it therefore rejects as coarse, and then of a world to which it does not yet belong and the prestigious characteristics of which it tries to appropriate. This places it in the position of a cultural consumer who wants to obtain models which he is incapable of producing for himself. This middle class is associated with a situation of vertical mobility, in which a growing number of the population tries to imitate it and picks up its reflexes. In this group individuals often have the conviction that they can become successful on their own through individual effort. This makes them sensitive to any form of individualized reassurance and is concealed in the variety of efforts made in an attempt to acquire appropriate cultural reactions (reading various types of popular scientific works, belonging to film clubs, etc.). It is through science that members of this group hope to achieve their personal ambitions. They can often only exercise this scientific control by means parallel to those of legitimate science, which they cannot enter on equal terms. This sometimes results in high status being given to involvement in para-scientific milieux (such as astrology), with which they are prepared to have a client relationship even if the use of the information it supplies is explicitly accepted only in the non-serious mode. This non-serious mode is opposed to the relations in the modes of the serious and the dramatic which most frequently characterize the forms of popular religion.

However this may be, even in its non-serious mode recourse to this language and these practices is based on scientific credibility. This credibility is then taken up into ambitions for regaining control of a universe which can be dominated by no other means. In a roundabout way, it is a use of the cultural model set up by modernity. In so far as this involves efforts to regain an individual balance, these practices cannot make any claim to social legitimacy. The situation is quite different with certain practices which try to form themselves into a sort of social movement, with some claim to replace the dominant legitimacies, and, for example, try to substitute a new social rationality for that of science. Is not this the explanation of the present success of Eastern mysticism, Yoga, drugs, eroticism and the search for activities to take one out of the triviality of everyday life? These practices, which are springing up all over the place, aim at a break with the dominant legitimacies and only after the event will we know if they have been successful. Here we are, to use Weber's language, in an area where prophecy and charisma are in competition with the priesthood for the conquest of legitimacy. The alternative movement proclaims the mystery without the occult; because of its desire for legitimacy it lays claim to publicity. On the contrary, the phenomenon which we have been describing has more in common with the sorcerer fixed in illegitimacy who makes no claim to overthrow the dominant legitimacy. In the same way, astrology, even if it has become mass astrology, does not imply the existence of an organized body promoting it and trying to overthrow astronomy. Astrology prospers without being ashamed of a client relationship with "magi" who present themselves as independent *entrepreneurs*. The modern occult, therefore, shares the rationality of the dominant culture and bases itself on the scientific approach and modernity, but in the form of compensation. Consequently it is the scientific rather than the religious world which will react against these appropriations which it rejects as invalid.

Fundamentally, modernity is a rejection of explicit sacrality, of the sacred which presents itself openly as such. It is also however a promotion, within the legitimacy of the scientific outlook, of the rationality of calculation and prediction and of the right to privacy. As a result, it is in relation to this content rather than to religious content that sacrality, including its occult forms, is developing.

The middle class, characterized by cultural insecurity and only partial control of the codes given high status by modernity, is likely to be very sensitive to the contradictions between the demands of modernity and its day-to-day experience. It is therefore prepared to interest itself in practices opposed to those encouraged by modernity. These opposed practices are, however, never the reverse of modernity, that is, they are not to be defined in relation to traditional religion, but in relation to the dominant features of modernity. The sacrality which develops as a result may therefore accentuate the marginal position of religion. These practices illustrate the fact that it is modernity which lays down the dominant criteria, and this can be seen from the fact that the world of religion does not feel directly threatened by these practices even if socially they are said to be semi-magical. If their opposition was directed towards the world of religion, this world would feel itself profaned. The absence of this feeling of profanation is a clear indication that it is not religious structures which are being inverted, and consequently that religion has lost weight as a factor in the formation of social legitimacy.

Translated by Francis McDonagh

Bas van Iersel

The Alternation of Secularizing and Sacralizing Tendencies in Scripture

I. A Steady Ebb and Flow?

IT IS difficult to say with certainty whether there is a steady ebb and flow between secularizing and sacralizing tendencies in Scripture for three main reasons. Firstly, the books cannot always be precisely dated. Secondly, they contain only partial information about man's religious experiences and his reflections about those experiences at any given period. Thirdly, we have only imperfect information about the relationship between these books and the various tendencies in Israel and the early Christian communities. This means that the conclusions drawn at the end of this article will inevitably be subject to great reservations.

Since other authors[1] have dealt with earlier parts of the Old Testament, in which desacralization is closely connected with Israel's liberation from the gods of the neighbouring nations,[2] I shall not discuss these sections, but limit myself to the books closer to the dividing line between the Old and New Testaments. As a New Testament scholar, I make no apology for dealing almost exclusively with these later Old Testament writings, since the

---

[1] See, for example, H. Renckens, "Geloof en religie in het Oude Testament", *Bijdragen, Tijdschrift voor Filofofie en Theologie*, 27 (1966), pp. 421 ff.; F. van Trigt, "Sekularisatie zo oud als de bijbel?", *Theologie en Pastoraat*, 68 (1972), pp. 28–39.

[2] W. von Soden, "Religiöse Säkularisierungstendenzen und Aberglaube zur Zeit der Sargoniden", *Studia Biblica et Orientalia*, III (*Analecta Biblica*, 12) (Rome, 1959), pp. 356–367; the author shows in this article how polytheism can lead to doubts which in turn result in secularization.

field is so enormous. The reader will have to turn to other authors for the New Testament.[3]

The books discussed here cover a period of some four hundred years—Job (500–400 B.C.), Chronicles, Ezra and Nehemiah (400–300), Ecclesiastes (300–250), Ecclesiasticus (190–117), Daniel (165 B.C.) and 1 and 2 Maccabees (ca. 100 B.C.). I believe that it is possible to detect an alternation between secularizing and sacralizing tendencies if these books are read in chronological order, although we cannot say that the authors were always reacting against the attitudes held by those who preceded them because they did not always come from the same circles. I shall therefore not deal with them in chronological order, but shall discuss firstly those books which tend to secularize faith and secondly the sacralizing books. There is, of course, no trace anywhere in the Old or New Testaments of any completely secularizing experience which completely excluded God.[4] What is meant by the terms secularization and sacralization in this context will become clear to the reader in the course of this article.

II. Job: God is not as Men say

Criticism was not unusual in Israel—the prophets condemned abuses in religious practice and attitudes especially (see, for example, Hos. 6. 6; Isa. 58; Jer. 7. 1–15). Job went much further. He could no longer believe in the traditional concept of God because of his experience as a man and therefore criticized the Old Testament "dogma" of God's retribution.

Job is contrasted with his friends, who are the custodians of the traditional teaching (Job 8. 8–10) and who know that God punishes evil with misfortune and rewards good with prosperity. Job used to believe this (29. 18–20; 30. 26), but the traditional doctrine cannot explain his terrible experience. The dialogues in the book are therefore strident with disbelief in the traditional

[3] For the New Testament, see H. Schürmann, "Neutestamentliche Marginalien zur Frage der 'Entsakralisierung' ", in *Der Seelsorger*, 38 (1968), pp. 38–48; 89–104; G. Every, "Sacralization and Secularization in East and West in the First Millennium after Christ", in *Concilium*, September 1969 (American Edn., Vol. 47); Every has almost nothing about the first century during the first millennium.

[4] This does not necessarily imply that Scripture should not be critically examined for evidence of complete secularization.

idea of God (see, for example, 9. 17, 22–24, 30–31; 19. 6–8; 21. 7–33; 27. 2), whom Job bitterly accuses of destroying both the blameless and the wicked (9. 22). Job's friends try to minimize his experience by their "dogma", but Job insists on the validity of his experience without losing his faith in God. His suffering tears him and his faith to pieces and he experiences God as his enemy (13. 24; 19. 11; 33. 10), but also as his saviour (19. 25).

Job is therefore not a book of God's absence, but one which emphasizes more than any other in the Bible that the traditional image of God is not proof against man's experience of reality. Job's attitude is secularizing because human experience is victorious over dogma. Faith, however, is victorious over human experience, so that the book is a classic example of a secularizing experience of faith.

It is important to note in this context that, whenever Job describes his own life in his own defence (see Job 31), he does not mention specific religious practices, but calls himself as it were a righteous humanist. It is not surprising, then, that the framework of the narrative, in which this portrait is retouched (Job 1–2; 42. 7–17), describes Job as a pious man who offered sacrifices (1. 5; 42. 8 ff.) and not only completely rehabilitates him but also presents him at the end as possessing twice as much as he possessed before his misfortune and as leading a long and happy life. The contrast between the man and the circumstances portrayed in this retouched framework and the man who rejects the traditional image of God is most striking.

III. ECCLESIASTES: GOD AS A WORD IN THE MARGIN OF EXISTENCE

Job expresses deep personal involvement. The "preacher", on the other hand, writes as a detached observer who goes against the prevailing optimism of the Wisdom literature, which he believes cannot be supported by the factual situation. His "all is vanity", repeated some twenty times, might better be translated as "it is all nothing". The preacher's pessimism is strengthened by his conviction that death, meaningless and absurd, strikes everyone and everything, the wise man and the fool, the righteous and the wicked, men and beasts alike: "For the fate of the sons of men and the fate of beasts is the same; as one dies, so dies another. They all have the same breath, and man has no advantage over the beasts; for all is vanity" (3. 19; see also 2. 12–17; 9. 2–3). After death, "all go to one place; all are from dust, and all turn to dust again. Who knows whether the spirit of man goes upward and the spirit of the beast goes down to the earth?" (3. 20). Not even the names of the dead survive—no one remembers them (1. 11; 2. 16; 9. 5, 15).

This pessimism is tempered by the author's sensitivity towards the little joys of life—eating and drinking, work (2. 24; 3. 12–13, 22; 4. 17–18; 8. 15; 9. 7) and life with the wife whom one loves (9. 9)—which are all that can enlighten the darkness of a life in which "all is vanity". The book that opens with the words "it is all nothing" ends with a list of counsels which opens with the words: "Rejoice, O young man, in your youth ... walk in the ways of your heart" (11. 9).

Despite his doubts about everything, the author is quite firm with regard to God (5. 1), who made everything (3. 11, 18; 7. 29) and has given man the "days of his life" and the little joys (5. 20), eating and drinking (3. 13), "wealth and possessions" (5. 19; 6. 2) and prosperity or adversity (7. 14). The author even relates the absurdity of life to God (3. 11–15; 8. 17; 11. 5) and advises his readers to go "to the house of God" (4. 17) as keeping a vow made to God (5. 3). He cannot therefore be regarded as a secularized man in the modern sense. But God seems to have been for him less meaningful than the little joys of life, little more than a word in the margin of existence, without any real part to play. For this reason, we may say that the secularizing tendency is present in his work even more strongly than in Job.

IV. ECCLESIASTICUS 38. 1–15:
GOD DURING THE HELLENISTIC "ENLIGHTENMENT"

The wisdom of Jesus Ben Sirach (or Ecclesiasticus) is, by contrast, optimistic, mainly because the author had a positive attitude towards the Hellenistic "Enlightenment" which emanated from the *Museon* at Alexandria, which had been in existence for about a century when the Hebrew text of Ecclesiasticus was written, probably in Jerusalem.[5] The results of the wide-ranging scientific

[5] See G. Sarton, *A History of Science. Hellenistic Science and Culture in*

research carried out at Alexandria were popularized, mainly by poets,[6] and this had a decisive effect on the Jews, many of whom forsook their own culture and religion and became convinced Hellenists. Although he was influenced by Hellenistic thought, Jesus Ben Sirach remained faithful to the traditional Jewish faith. This is especially clear from Ecclus. 44–50, in which the author praises the fathers of his faith and the high priest Simon, who had just died.

An example of the way in which he combines faith in God and acceptance of medical and pharmaceutical achievements of the Hellenistic "Enlightenment" is to be found in Ecclus. 38. 1–15. The doctor, the author insists, was created by God, who also makes the healing herbs grow and gives men the knowledge that they need to use these herbs to combat disease. The sick man should not simply pray and offer sacrifice, but also consult the doctor, whom he needs as much as he needs God. At times, Jesus Ben Sirach says, the doctor alone can bring about a cure, because he will pray to God to enable him to save life by his medicine.

Jesus Ben Sirach is shown in this passage to be an "enlightened" man who completely accepts the results of science. In this sense, he is undoubtedly secularized. His interpretation of the Torah is also enlightened in this way and, in the passage mentioned above, he is referring to Exod. 15. 25 when he says that God brings out of the earth medicines which the sensible man will not despise and that water was sweetened by the wood that Moses threw into it so that everyone could learn its strength. It is clear, then, that the author of Ecclesiasticus is a man steeped in the faith of the fathers, but at the same time progressive and open to Hellenistic culture and scientific achievements.

V. Chronicles, Ezra and Nehemiah:
The Primacy of the Ancient Dogmas

In order of time, the great historical work that includes 1 and 2 Chronicles, Ezra and Nehemiah should be placed between Job

---

the Last Three Centuries B.C. (Cambridge, 1959), pp. 29–34; 129–40; 400–12.
[6] *Op. cit.*, pp. 136–7.

and Ecclesiastes, because it originated round about 350 B.C., probably in Jerusalem. In sharp contrast to these two books, this historical work is marked by a strongly sacralizing tendency, expressed in at least four closely interconnected ways.

The first of these sacral characteristics is the prominence given to the dogma of retribution. Sin is shown to be the cause of misfortunes, such as the escape of chariots and horsemen (2 Chron. 16. 7–12), the loss of ships (20. 35–37), defeat, looting and death (24. 17–25; 25. 14–28) and leprosy (26. 16–23). An example of how the author of 2 Chron. moulded the facts to suit the dogma can be found in 2 Chron. 33. King Manasseh of Judah is completely condemned in 2 Kings 21, whereas the author of 2 Chron. suggests that Manasseh's journey to the King of Assyria was a deportation to Babylon as a punishment for promoting idolatry and that Manasseh repented there, was released and, on returning to Jerusalem, reigned well for many years. The author of 2 Chron. thus manipulated the historical facts to give support to a dogma and in this respect was very different in attitude from the "preacher" and from the author of Job.

In the second place, the author makes Yahweh intervene like a *Deus ex machina* in favour of Judah. Examples of such interventions are the victory against Jeroboam (2 Chron. 13. 13–20), the victory against the Cushites (14. 8–14) and above all Jehoshaphat's victory against the allied forces of Moab, Ammon and Seir (20. 1–30), all of which were the direct result of prayer.

Thirdly, the sacralizing tendency is quite clear from the author's exceptional interest in cultic matters. For example, he makes David bring the ark of the covenant from Kireath-Jearim before he begins to build a palace (1 Chron. 13), thus reversing the order of events in 2 Sam. 5–6. He also narrates in great detail David's preparations for the building of the temple (1 Chron. 22–29), in contrast to the books of Samuel and Kings, which give none of these details. The David of Chronicles seems to have been concerned with very little apart from cultic matters.

This is intimately connected with the fourth sacral characteristic of this historical cycle. David is presented not only as the founder of the temple cult in Jerusalem, but also as the model king of Judah at a time when the people were without a king and subject to the exclusive authority of the high priests. The author regarded this clerical leadership as no less hierocratic than the theocracy that prevailed at the time of David, which he accepted as the future norm.

The attitude found in Ezra and Nehemiah is very similar and we may say with confidence that this whole historical cycle bears witness to a powerfully sacralizing tendency.

VI. DANIEL'S CALL TO FAITHFULNESS TO THE "OLD-TIME RELIGION"

Daniel was written between 167 and 163 B.C., when Antiochus IV Epiphanus was persecuting the Palestinian Jews who refused to abandon the "old-time religion" and accept the Hellenistic view of life. Many Jews succumbed, but others remained faithful to the Law and it was these that the author aimed to encourage with the early history of Daniel and his companions at the Babylonian court. These faithful Jews were again and again saved from death and were also seen to be wiser than the Babylonian sages, with the result that even the king of Babylon eventually recognized the power of Yahweh.

In the second part of the book, the author heartens his readers by recounting and interpreting Daniel's visions, the fundamental message of which is that the sufferings of the persecuted Jewish community form part of God's meaningful plan of salvation. The day is approaching, the author proclaims through the visions of Daniel, when God will break the power of the pagan rulers and will establish his kingdom. The author of Daniel is also the first Old Testament writer to speak explicitly of the resurrection of the dead (12. 2–3). The apocalyptic style of narration and the frequent occurrence of angels show how strong the sacralizing tendency is in Daniel, but it is also clear that an insistence on real faith underlies this tendency.

VII. 1 AND 2 MACCABEES: GOD HELPS THOSE WHO ARE FAITHFUL TO HIS LAW

Faithfulness to the traditional religion is also the theme of 1 and 2 Maccabees, written between 110 and 63 B.C. and describing Jewish resistance to Hellenization and at the same time expressing a deep conviction that salvation can only come through keeping the Law (1 Macc. 2. 49–68). The author stresses that this was so in the past (see, for example, 14. 4–15) and that the one who in fact saves the faithful Jews is God, although his name is hardly mentioned in 1 Macc.

2 Macc. states explicitly what keeping the Law implies—circumcision (6. 10), observing the dietary (7) and the sabbath laws (15. 1–4) and participation in the temple cult (10; 14. 35–36). The relationship between keeping or failing to keep the Law and happiness or misfortune is also made explicit. God's grace follows observance of the Law, whereas disaster strikes the Jews when they turn away from God (4. 10–17). Jews who turn back to God are saved (7. 32–38). God helps those who offer sacrifice (3). Again, as in Daniel, the author is convinced that God will raise those who have died for the traditional faith to eternal life (7. 9, 14). Prayers and sacrifices are effective even in the case of those who have died after breaking the Law (12. 38–45). God's help in battle takes the form of a visible intervention by angels appearing as heavenly warriors winning the fight for the faithful Jews (3. 23–30; 10. 29–31; 11. 6–10), who in turn praise God as greater than Antiochus IV Epiphanes and call him *Kurios Epiphanes*, the Lord appearing in glory (15. 34).

Some of these ideas are comparable to those expressed in the Hellenistic type of historical writing of the period. Others are obviously influenced by emergent pharisaism. Taken as a whole, however, 1 and 2 Maccabees—and especially the latter—display a marked sacralizing tendency.

VIII. AN EBB AND FLOW BETWEEN SECULARIZATION AND SACRALIZATION?

To conclude that there is a steady ebb and flow between secularizing and sacralizing tendencies in these books would be to go a little too far. Several conditions would have to be satisfied before this conclusion can be justified. Firstly, we would have to know beyond any doubt that the texts present us with a true picture of the prevailing attitudes in an entire community or at least in a clearly defined section of that community. Secondly, the phenomenon of regular alternation between secularization and sacralization would have to be demonstrated over a fairly long period; and thirdly, we would have to have evidence that the successive documents describing these alternating tendencies were really the literary record of life in precisely the same community. Since these conditions cannot be fulfilled, we can only draw a few rather modest and cautious conclusions from our examination of these late Old Testament texts.

In the first place, it is clear from the texts that there was probably an alternating movement between a secular and a sacral experience of faith among the Palestinian Jews living between 500 and 100 B.C. This may have been the result of an inner dynamism or it may have been produced by external circumstances such as persecution. Even if there was no alternation, however, it cannot be denied that the two different attitudes existed and in this case they may both have been regarded as legitimate.

In the second place, there is no reason at all for us to conclude that the Jewish faith evolved from a sacral to a secular experience, the second marking a more advanced stage of development. Anyone claiming that sacralization was a retrogressive step would have to clarify the objective criteria on which he based this claim.

Finally, we are bound to conclude that faith is possible both in a sacral and in a secular experience of the living God—to some extent, these correspond to the two poles of a theocentric and an anthropocentric experience of God by man in the world.

Translated by David Smith

David Power

A Theological Perspective on
the Persistence of Religion

IN THIS essay, we shall first of all state the presuppositions which Christian theology makes in treating of the phenomenon of religion. In the second place, we shall indicate the questions which it can ask about this phenomenon. In the third place, the major part of the essay will deal with the conditions which are necessary if the Christian religion itself is to survive and propagate itself. Hopefully, it will become clear that treating of this last question is one way of dealing implicitly with several questions which touch on the religious phenomenon in general.

I. PRESUPPOSITIONS

When Christian theology considers the phenomenon of religion and religious practice in the world it takes its factual information and some theories from other sciences, such as comparative religion, anthropology, sociology and religious psychology. At the same time, it acts upon its own presuppositions in assessing this phenomenon and in relating questions about the persistence of religion to questions about Christianity itself.

As a working description, it may be accepted that religion is in its many different forms a complexity of beliefs and practices which expresses the meaning of life and the order of existence in terms of relationship to the sacred. It is not just a question of acknowledging the existence of the sacred, but one of establishing a relationship to it in practices and rites and of accepting a consequent ethic. Religion is as varied in its beliefs, practices and ethics as the notion of the sacred. Determining the meaning of the sacred and the alternation of the sacred and the secular depends on how one deals with the question of man's transcendence and of divine presence in the world—where divine presence is not necessarily taken to refer to a personal God. Depending on how one sees these issues, the sacred is conceived either as a separate sphere of human existence in which the requirements of the sacred world are satisfied or as a distinctive dimension of the whole of reality.

Even within Christianity itself, there are different approaches to the question of the sacred and the alternation of the sacred and the secular. At the same time, Christianity will presuppose that "genuine religion always involves worship of what is genuinely ultimate. Religion, worship and ultimate reality are thus indissolubly related."[1]

Christian theology will also make some distinction between faith and religion. It is not one which is easy to delineate, since the distinction is not between two wholly separate realities but necessarily allows for a relationship between the two. In general, faith can be understood as the interiorization of a meaning, the inner response of man to an expressed meaning, presented by another. It involves a personal relationship and a commitment to the other person. Religion is the mediation of faith, as well as its expression and its support, in teaching, ritual, institution and behaviour. The greatest difficulty here is to distinguish between those expressions which are essential to faith in religion, and those which are variable because subject to different cultural influences. This variability in religious expression is necessary to the mediation of faith, since it is presented to people who belong to different cultural backgrounds and environments.

II. What Theology asks about Religion

A reflective Christian theology can ask five questions about the phenomenon of religion:

1. What does Christian revelation itself have to say about the

---

[1] Carl G. Vaught, "Two Concepts of God", in *Religious Studies* 6 (1970), p. 221.

nature of the God-man relationship which points to the necessity and permanence of religion?

2. What is the possible salvific value of non-Christian religions?

3. What are the criteria by which religious authenticity may be judged?

4. Why does religion often take on imperfect and at times even debased forms and survive in these forms?

5. What are the conditions that authentic religion, and in particular Christian religion, may endure and propagate itself?

These five questions follow one another in a logical sequence, as we shall now show. The Christian symbol-system, in its kerygmatic proclamation, its mythical[2] presentation and interpretation (as contained especially in the Scriptures), its community order, its sacramental celebration and its ethical demands, points to the fact that faith and beliefs[3] cannot be imparted and cannot survive without religion. This total symbolic complexity is necessary that the God-man relationship may be possible and that faith may act as a force in men's lives. None of these elements can be explained simply as the consequence of a positive divine law, laying down the conditions of Christian obedience, and which could just as easily have been otherwise. Whether we take the form of the presentation of the message in the Scriptures, or the sacramental system, or the community order, or the conduct required of those who believe in Christ, each has its own intrinsic intelligibility and its own inner structure, which allows it to serve as an appropriate medium for the communication and expression of faith. The cultural elements which finally determine these factors have to be taken into account, and are not always that easily discernible, but without some similar symbolic system we know that faith would be rendered humanly impossible. The inner core and basic adherence to meaning of any religious system requires a similar complexity of factors to mediate it and keep it alive.

[2] Mythical does not mean untrue, but refers to the literary form in which the message is expressed.

[3] Beliefs are not as fundamental as faith and do not affect the core of meaning found in a religion. Thus the existence of angels may constitute a belief for some Christians, but is not an essential part of the faith.

On the other hand, Christian revelation speaks to us of the love of a personal God for the world, of Christ as the focal point and transformation of history and the beginning of a new creation, of the presence of the Spirit in the world as the operative force of faith and salvation, and of the transcendence of man in his nature and God-given finality. Faith in such a triune reality of God's self-communication to man is impossible without religion, and so the knowledge itself of God's love makes us certain that religion will endure as the necessary medium of faith and love. The knowledge of this love also explains why religion undergoes periodic reform and revival, and enables us to accept the work of propheticism in bringing about such reform as the action of God's Spirit. Pushed far enough, confidence in the presence of Christ and his Spirit in the Church may have at one time given rise in theology to an optimism about the spread of Christianity and a severe attitude towards other religions. But theology is bound to reflect upon facts, as well as upon the sources of tradition, and in face of the comparative provincialism of the Christian religion theologians in more recent times have begun to ask whether the loving God may not use the medium of other religions for his communion with man. In other words, they have begun to inquire into the possible salvific value and into the significance of non-Christian religions.

Since religion also exists in imperfect, or even debased forms, to look for God's action through other religions makes it necessary to work out criteria whereby we can assess the authenticity of religious beliefs, practices and systems, i.e., the real value which they may have in permitting man to commune with the transcendent and loving God, and to worship that which is genuinely ultimate. But since religion sometimes takes on forms which are degrading, or since it can exclude the existence of a personal God, one does not explain the endurance of religion simply by saying that God's presence in the world by his Spirit assures this. Besides setting the criteria whereby we can judge a religion's authenticity, is it possible to explain why it survives even when it can hardly be said to serve as a medium of communication with God?

Some basis for this is found in the fact that religion deals with the problems of life and death, and with the anxieties of man's relations to community and to the powers which he cannot control. This is true even of genuine religions, which combine an answer to these problems with the worship of a personal God. When it loses its vision of a loving God, religion may still exist as a way of dealing with these anxieties, particularly anxiety about the presence of the sacred in life, about human suffering or failure, and above all about death. In such cases, the element of faith is missing from religion, but the meaning offered resides in such things as the placation of spirits, hope for preternatural help, the search for some action or some area of human life, such as sexual love, in which the essential core of meaning is posited. Whether it turns out to be a tranquillizer or a challenge in face of these problems, is one good criterion for distinguishing a genuine from an imperfect religion, since a religion which takes account of a personal, loving and saving God places demands upon the believer to take issue with questions of ultimate meaning and to commit himself to an ethic that takes the religious affirmation seriously. Sometimes the concern with one's own human problems, or the community's problems, is dominant in religious practice so that it survives principally as a way of allaying anxiety, and the real challenge is avoided. If this remains the uppermost concern, then it is bound to take on many superstitious and debased forms. On the other hand, by focusing on the problem of human living it may awaken the need for ultimate concern and meaning and thus be a means of opening up to the perspective of faith. The Christian symbol system incorporates these problems into its kerygma and sacramental universe. It has its own way of answering them, but we cannot be surprised that even when the Christian answer is discarded, or any answer which takes in faith in a loving and saving God, religion survives as a way of dealing with these problems.

If we deal more elaborately with the last of our five questions, i.e., the conditions for the persistence and propagation of religious systems, and pay particular attention to Christianity itself in this regard, this is because we are thus implicitly dealing with the four preceding questions as well. The biggest problem which faces Christianity in the Western world today is that of remaining viable in a changing cultural environment and of dealing with the crisis of faith which necessarily ensues when the whole manner of its expression is subjected to flux.[4] This means that in surveying the conditions under which Christianity may take on suitable religious forms in and for this new situation we are talking about conditions under which any religion may persist in an authentic way. To appreciate the difficulties which Christianity faces in keeping its faith vital in the course of a cultural transition is by the same token a help towards understanding why it has largely remained a Western phenomenon. The failure to meet the cultural challenge involved in taking on the aspects of non-European civilizations can be accounted to a deficiency inherent in the Christian religion itself.[5]

III. The Conditions for a Christian Religion which mediates Faith

These conditions can be listed and explained as follows:

1. An authentic Christian expression treats of life and death, evil, sin, personal worth and community belonging, of reconciliation and brotherhood among men. The fear of death, the clinging to and guilt of sin, the anxiety about personal worth and the disruption of human community, with their opposites, the hope of life, the desire for grace and pardon, the desire to be loved and to be able to love, the search for brotherhood, and the awe of the holy which somehow influences the doings of this world, constitute the fundamental human experience in which religion is grounded. This is what it transforms into a meaningful reality, in which these fears are conquered and these hopes fulfilled. Even though it may possess an apparent nobility, a religion which has nothing to say about these factors of human existence will eventually be ignored.

It is also possible that a religion may choose to isolate some one factor and, by concentrating on it and putting all man's hopes in it, blind its adherents to more fundamental questions.

[4] On the changing conditions of religious expression, cf. B. Lonergan, "Theology in its New Context", in L. K. Shook, ed., Theology of Renewal 1 (New York, 1969), pp. 34-46.
[5] One may here distinguish between the Christian religion and the truth of the Christian kerygma. Religion is the whole complex by which faith is expressed, grows and is mediated, and so it is much influenced by diverse cultural elements.

This happened in some ancient religions, which relied too much on sexual experience, and even on ritual sex, as an answer to man's need for life and happiness. Ancient religions which betrayed this interest in sex none the less retained or developed their mythologies about the gods. Some modern sexual behaviour has its own ritual aspect, and one can find such things as celebrations and rituals of love in which the stress is on sexual expression, and in which such love, without any reference to a world of the gods, is taken to be the answer to man's woes.

Christian religion on its part has often erred in the opposite extreme with regard to sexual love and treated it as something to be feared or looked down upon. Its betrayal of its followers can consist in the isolation of other elements of the Christian message or undue attention to some one particular human problem, with the consequent loss of a total vision. This happens, for example, if in practice Christianity encourages resignation to sorrow without its counterpart of courage and hope, if it denies personal worth by subordinating the individual to the communality or religious system, or if on the other extreme it turns religion into a purely individualistic affair. It can also adopt one or other of the extremes of Pelagianism or Puritanism in face of sin, or falsify the nature of death and the hope of the resurrection by too material a concern with the life of the new creature who emerges from the transforming power of death in Christ. A genuine Christian practice keeps the balance between the hope in the resurrection and the way of the folly of the cross.

2. Authentic Christianity, it follows, keeps the personal element of religion in the foreground. The unique element of the Christian faith is the revelation of the personal God who is Father, the cosmic lover who asks for the response of love and thus promises union. This is falsified whenever Christian practice loses the sense of response, if it becomes too centred on human development and forgets that "God first loved us" and that all that we do is the glorification of God, if it makes God into a lawgiver instead of a saviour and a father, if it does not foster the interiorization of the word and the law and the love of God in Christ through the Spirit, if it becomes a superstition to deal with the troubles of life on the basis of a false notion of

providence instead of developing a way of living which is response to God's love.

3. To be truly integrated into the life of any people or civilization, Christian faith needs to receive a poetic and symbolic expression which is indigenous to the culture, not foreign to it. This applies to ritual, celebrations of every sort, devotions, art in its different forms, or in other words to every expression of the faith which appeals to the affective and seeks to make it a living force which involves the totality of the human person and to develop the intersubjective relationships of the community on a basis of Christian vision and mission.

The language of kerygma, of catechesis, of mystagogy, of worship, in short all the symbols of a religion, are very much charged with cultural elements, because they are the ways in which religion presents its message as an answer to and a transformation of the human experience of a given people or culture. What an authentic religion tries to do is to transform, not to contradict, human experience and its various expressions. Faith must speak through these religious symbols, and a people develops and grows in its faith, and discovers all the consequences and further meaning of its faith, through them.

Credal expression itself takes in cultural elements and uses symbolic language. It is not a purely objective expression which presents the articles of faith to be accepted by all. In facing cultural transition, one of the difficulties of the messenger of the faith is to discern the objective content which has to be kept intact, as well as the expressions which are conditioned by a culture, or by a particular problematic which belongs to a given time or place.

Elements of revelation and faith can somehow be present in a non-Christian or in a profane culture. When discovered, these are respected and may serve as media of a fuller faith commitment. Old Testament and Christian revelation was not in the first place a matter of introducing entirely extraneous elements into the lives and practices of the Semitic or Hellenistic peoples. Revelation was often the inner light which allowed a people to perceive the full implication and potential of an event or of given beliefs and practices. It gave a people the possibility to pass through and transcend a given stage in their religious experience and to come to a greater awareness of God and his love for his people.

In presenting Jesus Christ in new cultural conditions, the question is how far we can present him as God's answer to the aspirations of, and the already existent awareness of the sacred present in that culture. Jesus said of himself that he had come to fulfil, not to abolish, the Law and the prophets. The fulfilment was not just an addition to what they already said. It was a perfecting of the faith-experience of God which the Jews who had interiorized the Law and the prophets already possessed. Granted the singular nature of Jewish religious history and of its special relation to Christ, something analogous could be said about the faith-experience of a transcendent power which any people has attained through its religious expression, or even through its fidelity to its profane commitments when these involve brotherhood and respect for the potentialities of human life.

To use the poetic, symbolic and ritual expressions of a culture to mediate Christian faith requires dialogue, in which several questions are involved. How does a people give voice to its feelings and aspirations when these concern the religious problems of which we have already spoken? What is its reaction to traditional Christian symbols, and how far can these be used to transform human experience in this new setting? How far can an authentic Christian faith be expressed in symbols taken from a new culture? Or how can a developing culture express its faith in new symbols? Involved in this inquiry is the question of the existence of universal symbols that can find resonance in any cultural setting and the extent to which some of the basic Christian symbols, such as the water-symbolism of baptism or the eucharistic meal, belong in this category.

One point worthy of particular note is the approach to a culture's cosmology, or in other words its vision of the universe. Many cultures and religions see the world peopled by spirits of various sorts, or by dynamic forces. This is their symbolic way of expressing their relation to the universe, its mysteriousness and their own limitations and possibilities in entering into communion with it. It also expresses their sense of the sacred or of the divine which is present in the universe and of its part in human affairs as far as these involve some attempt to control man's surroundings and his own life as it depends for development upon the environment in which he lives. When faced with such a vision of things, which leaves room for the symbolism of spirits, Christian preaching can either contradict it or turn it into a theophany. The Semitic peoples who were called to be the people of the one true God lived in a world peopled with spirits. This persuasion sometimes led them into idolatry, but on the other hand it formed the basis for the angelology of the Old Testament. In later times, Christianity often misunderstood this angelology and gave too literal an interpretation to the talk about the angels, whereas in Old Testament times and in some Eastern Christian rites (where, for example, Christ and the Holy Spirit are called angels, or where the angels are invoked to conjure up the reverence due to God's majesty) angels were a kind of divine revelation, a way of expressing God's own mysterious nearness to his people. It was a way of coupling a sense of awe before the transcendence of God with a sense of his gracious nearness in love. The approach to other peoples who symbolize their relations with the cosmos and the sacred in the figures of spirits can surely learn something from this.

In its present phase of cultural development, the Western world is increasingly convinced of the independence of the secular and finds it hard to cope with stories of miracles, saints or special divine interventions. At the same time, it has its own need of the sacred and its own need of evincing its awe of the universe—even though it is now possible to travel to the moon and contact other planets. To persist in a symbolic and devotional expression which makes miracles and saints and special divine interventions necessary would spell the ruin of Christian religion, even if such language were still attractive to some people. Some would reject a religion which postulated such beliefs, but even those who accepted them would inevitably experience an inner tension and conflict between their theories and technical knowledge of the universe and its forces on the one hand and their symbolic expression of their relation to it on the other. Philosophy and theology have already responded to this new awareness by developing a theory of the sacred and the secular which emphasizes the sacred and the transcendent as a dimension of reality rather than as a separate sphere of existence, and speaks of fidelity to the profane as an opening out to the sacred. What is still lacking is a new symbolism, which allows man to encounter God simultaneously with his grasp of the universe and the particulars in it, a ritual and a prayer expression which is a discernment of the divine presence in human life and history and a challenge to a response in faith, which channels all human drives, affective as well as intelligent.

4. Without a witness of life on the part of its disciples, a religion cannot succeed. This constitutes the spiritual and living experience which is communicated through religious practices, and is the ultimate factor which makes religion credible. The Christian gospels always insisted on this sign of credibility and on the existence of the community of charity into which new members are incorporated. Faith is interpreted and presented in word and symbol, but by that same token the word and symbol are an interpretation of the works in which faith shows its vitality. What is shared with others is faith in God as the Father of the Lord Jesus Christ, the charity which unites, the personal relation to God and Christ, the sense of the Spirit, the experience of what this means for the problems of good and evil, life and death, meaningful involvement in the world coupled with the hope of the future. It is also prayer, in its religious ritual and its ultimate quality of contemplation. Today, what is needed more than anything is the witness of involvement in the needs of the world and in the transformation of society, without any loss of faith in God and without any devaluation of contemplation as the truest end which man can pursue in this life.

5. Besides its witness and its symbolic expression, religion also needs its institutions, i.e., its forms of government and organization, and its law which regulates relations among its followers and adherents. The institutional element of Christianity is still the subject of controversy between churches, and among members within single churches. It is an important question in a stage of cultural transition, because the view taken of these structures makes all the difference between attempts at adaptation and a more radical reform, in the strong sense of that word. There seems to be a growing realization that the institutional factor in Christianity is less a matter of the institutions formed by Jesus Christ or the apostles as a necessary means for the com-

munication of his word and grace, than a question of the forms most apt to express the community self-awareness in a given time and place, in continuity with a past Christian tradition. The nature of the Church is that of a community which is one with Jesus Christ through faith and charity, the body which through his Spirit is identified with him and is his sacramental presence in the world. Not only are the spiritual values primary in the sense that they are the most important, but also in the sense that they precede the institutions. The role which the institutions play is to support the spiritual values, of which they are in the first instance the expression. They depend for their credibility and permanence, or at least for their efficaciousness, on the continuing relationship with these values. A divorce can and often has occurred between the institution and the value of which it was originally the expression, and yet the institution has lived on in its historical form, simply because it was there to begin with, and there is an innate conservatism in any community which promotes past structures. This divorce occurs either because the community's self-awareness in faith changes or modifies the sense of values, or because there is a corruption within the institution and it maintains the form without the spirit. In either case, the result is that the institution is no longer supported by the spirit of the community and is not an apt instrument whereby to promote the expression of faith in any of its religious practices or in its works.[6]

There is need today for institutional reform, in both non-Western and Western countries, and the same changes cannot hold good for every part of the world. To take only the example of the Western crisis, an authoritarian institution, which is sometimes also unevangelical in its style of life, cannot support the values of a Christian community which has come to a greater awareness of the co-responsibility of its members in the mission of Christ. The forms of government, priesthood and law need to be configured to the sense of mission. This sense of mission is the product of Christian faith in a cultural environment which encourages participation. It would be naïve to simply state that the

[6] For several examples of this, cf. Y. Congar, "Renewal of the Spirit and Reform of the Institution", Concilium, March 1972 (American Edn., Vol. 73), pp. 39–49.

Christian faith which comes to us from the New Testament indicates a community which through the working and charism of the Spirit accepts the responsibility of all its members for the life and mission of the Church, and thus claim that in fostering co-responsibility we are returning to a purer Christian ideal. Such an explanation fails to take account of other cultural influences, and of the ultimate fact that faith as a response to God in Christ works within a community which is subject to the influences of a given culture, causing this community to find its own response to God in Christ within that culturally determined situation. It is indeed true that in New Testament times there was a strong sense of the presence of the Spirit, as the inner anointing which every Christian received to interiorize the word of Christ, and that this led to a respect for the distinctive contribution of different charisms. It is also true that a loss of this sense of the Spirit was one of the factors which led to a growing separation between clergy and faithful. None the less, we cannot either forget that today in the Western world faith commands a response from Christian communities in which the cultural influence urges people to a greater sense of sharing and participation, and in which this contribution is possible because of standards of education and pluriformity in skills which prevail in our society. This of itself demands new forms of law, institution and obedience. The ultimate Christian obedience is to the word of God. The immediate obedience is to the forms of expression which this word takes, but they must be forms apt to communicate. This holds for law and institutions, as well as for other ways of expression.

6. Without historical consciousness, none of these changes in religious expression is possible, whether it be a change in symbolic expression, in creed, in ritual, in devotion, in institutions, or in life-style. Historical consciousness[7] is aware of the creativity of faith and of the cultural differences within which this creativity takes place. It knows that faith is not a formulation which has to be couched in certain terms, but a constantly growing response of the believing community to the Christ-event, an event

[7] On the nature and relevancy of historical consciousness, cf. J. W. O'Malley, "Reform, Historical Consciousness, and Vatican II's Aggiornamento", in *Theological Studies* 32 (1971), pp. 573–601.

whose intelligibility and potentiality can never be exhausted. Faith then creates its own religious expression, but according to the needs and the cultural sense of the believer. Historical consciousness does not deny the continuity which comes from Christian tradition or from the common nature which all men possess, but it avoids too many *a priori* answers in setting the boundaries of continuity.

7. Finally, a systematic reflection is a guide to every religion, and for Christianity this means a reflective theology. An indigenous theology, be it Western or otherwise, is based on a knowledge and explanation of the world of interiority of a people and its culture. This comprises the values, the modes of communication and self-expression, the ways of thought proper to a culture. To come to know it, it is necessary to develop a philosophical anthropology which comes from a reflection upon experience, both internal and external, both personal and dialogal. This enables a people to meet the demands of theory in grounding and explaining the faith-experience, and assures that there is no hiatus between the symbolic, devotional and institutional on the one hand, and the quest for truth on the other, but rather grants them internal coherence in the mind of the community and its individual members. Scholasticism sought such a theology for the West in the past and modern theologians are seeking it for the newly emerging Western culture. The same needs to be done for non-European cultures.

IV. Conclusion

If the Christian religion is the constant process of creativity which needs to meet the conditions explained here, this is true in its own way of any authentic religion. Authentic religion to endure must so pursue ultimate reality that it does not exclude or render impossible faith in a personal God.[8] It also needs the

[8] It is not here possible to discuss the nature of Christian dialogue with those world religions which express their pursuit of ultimate reality in terms which are non-personal. The question for the Christian is: to what extent do they open up the possibility of faith in a loving, personal God? How does the pursuit of ultimate reality serve and develop the transcendental openness of man which eventually brings him into communion with God? This could be stated, in other words, as that respect for human

credible witness of its adherents and respect for its religious tradition, as well as the cultural expression of faith in a symbol system, an institution and a reflection. This cultural expression, as it is renewed or newly formed, itself adds to the religious tradition, but it remains continuous with earlier tradition because of the original sources, because of respect for history, and because of the common humanity which has the same universal needs and tendencies.

The Christian is convinced that religion will survive, because he is convinced that God continues to communicate himself in love to man. He is also conscious that not all religion is authentic and that the Christian religion itself must undergo constant purification and development. In a sense, the religious response in which faith is embodied is always a response to a call similar to that which God made to Abraham: "Go from your country and your kindred and your father's house to the land that I will show you" (Gen. 12. 1).

---

transcendence which does not cause man to stop short at limited objects, but evokes an ongoing development, such that it eventually leads men to an encounter with the personal God, however this may be conceptually stated.

John Shea

The Second Naïveté:
Approach to a Pastoral Problem

I. The Problem of Meaningless Religious Language

MOST local churches consider that their pastoral problems centre around service and witness. Is the Church witnessing to the Gospel and is it serving other people? These two overall concerns splinter into a hundred practical questions. Is the school facilitating and encouraging the Christian way of life? How should the money be budgeted? How many people is the Church reaching in the neighbourhood? Are the aged being cared for? Are the sick being ministered unto? Are the youth being given strong yet understanding structures for growth? Is something being done about the quality of family life? Are emotional problems being recognized and dealt with? Is the liturgy appealing? Are the sacraments being administered? How and to what extent is the Church engaging in political activity? From the firm base of Christian belief the energies of the local church move outward to heal and minister.

In recent years many local churches have experienced an internal pastoral problem which threatens to overwhelm these outward concerns. This problem, which is often more felt than defined, goes by many names. It has been called "the identity crisis", "the inbreak of secularism", "the irrelevance of religion", or simply "lack of faith". But perhaps the most accurate diagnosis of this uneasiness at the heart of Church life is that for many people religious language has become meaningless. The Christian symbols which once articulated the Church's faith and directed and motivated its activities have lost their power. They no longer positively energize the style of Church life because they no longer enthral and persuade with their overwhelming grasp of the real. This is not just the perennial problem of the interplay of faith and doubt. To use temporarily the distinction of linguistic philosophy between meaning and truth, the pastoral problem concerns more the meaning of the Christian symbols than their truth. In other words the churchman does not easily and immediately understand how the religious language he uses fits into the world he experiences. As one senior citizen said about the Christian symbols, "They no longer taste real".

Although this problem of meaningless religious language is often ignored, it has a pervasive influence on the style of Church life. Nowhere is this more evident than in the Sunday homily. The traditional symbols of faith—sin, grace, the Kingdom of God, creation, the Spirit—no longer seem to have a dominant role in preaching. Preaching has found new and more convincing words in the psychoanalytic vocabulary—growth, relationship, response, defensiveness, openness, etc. These words may be legitimate attempts to interpret one aspect of the Christian symbols. But the point is that they are not understood as interpretations but as substitutes. The symbols do not act as touchstones for homiletic reflection. They are bypassed in favour of a more serviceable rhetoric. Not only preaching but Church activities in general betray the confusion and embarrassment which surrounds religious language. In conversation religious symbols are barriers to communication. People talk around them, over them, under them, but never through them. The meaning of symbols are not immediately recognized. They do not bind people together in common affirmation and destiny but reduce them to awkward silence. Perhaps in the area of personal and liturgical prayer the meaningless of religious language is most acutely felt. Dialogue with a personal God, once a smooth and natural thing, is now highly suspect. In the words of Kazantzakis, "I once thought God laughed and wept and fought by my side but now I feel I've talked to my own shadow." At liturgy the verbal interaction of the Father, Son and Spirit leave people confused. What does it mean to ask the Father to send the Spirit to change these gifts into the Body and Blood of his Son? Given this confusion about religious symbols the local church often leans towards what is more certain—a counselling clinic or a social programme. But unless the meaning of religious symbols is recovered, the Church will lose its specific religious roots and transcendent calling.

In the conclusion of *The Symbolism of Evil* Paul Ricoeur offers a model to interpret this pastoral crisis of religious symbols.[1] He posits a movement in man's relationship to his religious symbols from a primitive to a second naïveté. For pre-modern man, Ricoeur holds, there existed an immediacy of belief, a flush-tight relationship to religious symbols, a primitive naïveté. But modern man, precisely because he is modern, is a critical creature. He is informed by philology, exegesis, phenomenology of religion, the psychoanalysis of language. Although each modern man may not be personally aware of these disciplines, they form the cultural matrix out of which he thinks and acts. Consequently he does not have an immediate and undifferentiated rapport with the symbols of faith. They do not spontaneously disclose for him the sacred and lead him to the experience of God. For modern man primitive naïveté has been irrevocably lost. But it is Ricoeur's contention that modern man is able to inhabit his religious symbols in a second naïveté. This second naïveté is not achieved by the creation and maintenance of an isolated world faith but precisely in and through criticism. To recover his inherited symbols modern man must place himself in the hermeneutical circle. Bluntly stated this circle is "We must understand in order to believe, but we must believe in order to understand".[2] Through critical interpretation religious symbols will regain their power and become transparent to the sacred. Modern man then must not remain detached but believe in the symbols and live with them. He wagers that in his commitment to the symbols he will have "a better understanding of man and of the bond between the being of man and the being of all beings".[3] If modern man had to understand in order to believe, he must now believe in order to fully understand. Paul Ricoeur's model diagnoses the "felt need" of many local churches. Church people are caught

[1] This paper does not attempt to analyse the philosophical anthropology of Paul Ricoeur or follow faithfully his hermeneutical methodology. It only hopes to use the skeletal structure of a "second naïveté" to interpret and guide a particular pastoral problem.

[2] Paul Ricoeur, *The Symbolism of Evil* (Boston, 1967), p. 351.

[3] *Ibid.*, p. 355.

between a primitive and second naïveté. They can neither retreat to an undifferentiated, non-critical relationship to the symbols of their faith nor can they advance to a second and more creative relationship. Today's churchman wants desperately to be called again by the symbols of the sacred. In order for this to happen he must move through the "desert of criticism",[4] to listen to the insights of science, psychology, sociology and history, in an initial step towards understanding.

II. Contemporary Critiques of Religious Symbols

The rise and tremendous success of the natural and physical sciences has forced religion into a new self-understanding. In the conflict with science religion has become aware that its language is not literal but symbolic and that it is concerned not with a neutral account of the observable world but an interpretation of the transcendent dimension of human experience. At one time the mythic-symbolic language of religion functioned both as a scientific explanation and as a statement of ultimate concern. Over the last four hundred years religious language has been gradually purged of its scientific pretensions. In the battle between biblical creation and evolution and between cataclysmic geology and uniformitarianism it became clear that the language and truth of religion was radically different from that of science. Science attempted to talk impartially about the interaction of objects "out there": religion talks passionately about the depth of human existence and the meaning of history. But this distinction is difficult to maintain and teach when the prevailing spirit of the age is positivism. The scientific mode of knowledge is popularly considered the only way to the real. This cultural mood induces a flat-minded literalism where religious symbols are not allowed to function symbolically but are frozen into statements about an ontological deity. They do not configure and mobilize human experience but are considered solely as independent entities susceptible to detached scrutiny. In this way religious symbols are victimized into literal language designating invisible objects. For most people religious language is a form of "supernatural positivism". The first step to a second naïveté is away from a literal

4 *Ibid.*, p. 349.

understanding of religious language and towards an awareness of the relationship between symbol and experience.

The critiques of psychology, sociology and history converge to emphasize the relativity and cultural indebtedness of the religious symbol. The social science approach is to examine symbols as projections of the individual and social order. In the individual order religious symbols are sublimations of repressed impulses (Freud). For example the symbol of a Father God is traced back and explained by a primordial murder of the father by the sons and the consequent guilt this induced. In the social order religious symbols are disguised ideologies (Marx). They are consciously or unconsciously the tools of exploitation and dominance. From the historical perspective symbols become understandable and explainable by the cultural circumstances in which they originated. Psychology, sociology and history may bring a deeper understanding of religious symbolism but they do not bring an exhaustive explanation. It is true that the symbol possesses projective elements from the personality of both the individual and the society and that its historical context is the clue to its meaning but these insights do not "play out" the religious symbol. Religious symbolism must be encountered on its own terms. Mircea Eliade has stated well the unique, non-reductionistic quality of the religious symbol: "A religious phenomenon will only be recognized as such if it is grasped at its own level, that is to say, if it is studied as something religious. To try to grasp the essence of such a phenomenon by means of physiology, psychology, sociology, economics, linguistics, or any other study is false; it misses the one unique and irreducible element in it—the element of the sacred."[5]

Presupposed in the reductionistic criticisms of science, psychology, sociology and history is an historical-evolutionary model of man. Comte's theory of age displacement is still subtly at work. Symbolic mythological language belongs to the childhood of man. Whatever insight and wisdom that language once contained can now be taken up and clarified in more scientific terms. But a more suitable model than displacement is differentiation. In the modern age man has not outgrown symbolic language, he has

[5] Mircea Eliade, *Patterns in Comparative Religion* (Cleveland and New York, 1958), p. xiii.

merely distinguished it from the empirical and the descriptive. Symbolic language has a perennial place in human conversation because it reaches into the depths of human experience to express the perceptions and feelings of man about the whole order of existence into which he fits. As symbolic language cannot perform the necessary literal function so literal language cannot perform the necessary symbolic function. Religious symbols reach down and gather up the dimension of ultimacy in human experience. They are always particularized, stemming from a certain historical milieu and reflecting the individual and societal personality. But also and distinctively they have a fundamental grasp on the sacred, a primordial hold on being. If modern man can, through criticism, live within these symbols, he will once again experience the sacred. In the modern age religious symbols cannot be believed in, they must be believed through. The goal of the symbol is not to bring man information but to lead him to experience. When religious symbols become both a revelation and a guide to the transcendent dimension of experience, they will regain their power to direct and motivate Christian life.

III. THE TRANSCENDENT DIMENSION OF EXPERIENCE

Many critics charge that the greatest crime of technological society is that it alienates man from himself. All experiences are standardized. Joys and sorrows are suffered automatically and accompanied by the great levelling remark, "That's the way life is". Attention is constantly centred on gadgets which encourage man to ask a hundred technical questions but which restrict him from asking the question of existence itself. If man is to recover the meaning of his religious symbols, he must break the hardened formulations which limit his awareness. He must place a stethoscope on his experiences and find there the beatings which are vital to his life but which he often overlooks. In short he must become sensitive to the transcendent dimension of experience which calls him to go beyond his present understanding and development. At the heart of this awareness of transcendence is what Michael Murphy calls "the feeling of being entered by, or entering upon, something greater . . .".[6]

[6] Michael Murphy, "Education for Transcendence", *Transcendence*, ed. Herbert Richardson and Donald R. Cutler (Boston, 1969), p. 18.

The experience of transcendence needs to be demystified. Unfortunately in the churches the model for transcendence has often been ecstatic union—Paul in the seventh heaven, Francis on Mount Alverno, Joseph of Cupertino floating through a church. With this model the transcendent becomes a synonym for the esoteric and the bizarre. But these ecstasies—assuming that they are valid—are only the most intense and spectacular form of transcendent experience. Transcendence can be a more common, quieter, but no less real experience. It is often described as a feeling of union, a sense of the whole, of standing outside oneself, of life purified and renewed, of satisfaction and joy. Man comes into contact with the More, the Mystery, the Whole, the Encompassing. Transcendent experience can be triggered by just about anything but some of the more common contexts are nature, sexual love, the birth of a child, religious liturgies, great works of art, scientific knowledge, poetry, creative endeavour, the beautiful. Transcendent experiences are what Ian T. Ramsey calls "cosmic disclosures", situations where the Universe "comes alive", where a "dead", "dull", "flat" existence takes on "depth" or another "dimension".[7] The psychologist Abraham Maslow thinks that peak experiences will be the distinguishing factor between two future types of religious personality. ". . . All or almost all people have or can have peak experiences. . . . To sum it up . . . the two religions of mankind tend to be the peakers and the non-peakers, that is to say, those who have private, personal, transcendent, core religious experiences easily and often and who accept them and make use of them, and, on the other hand, those who have never had them or who repress or suppress them and who, therefore, cannot make use of them for their personal therapy, personal growth, or personal fulfillment."[8] When a man becomes aware of the transcendent dimension of his experience, he reaches for a language to express and interpret it. The language available is religious symbolism.

Although there are no occasions which cannot disclose the transcendent dimension of life (witness Whittaker Chambers' re-

[7] Ian T. Ramsey, "Talking About God: Models, Ancient and Modern", *Myth and Symbol*, ed. F. W. Dillistone (London, 1966), p. 87.

[8] Abraham Maslow, "Religious Aspects of Peak Experiences", *Personality and Religion*, ed. William Sadler, Jr. (New York, 1970), p. 179.

flections of God while watching his daughter's cut hair fall into her ear), certain situations have traditionally been more conducive. The limit situations of birth and death force man into wonder and terror about the larger mystery which brings him into earthly existence and which takes him out. The basic experiences of wonder, trust, love, joy, sorrow, hope and despair plunge man, sometimes agonizingly, into transcendent awareness. In situations of freedom and power and autonomy men often feel a higher responsibility, a deeper commitment. Michael Novak names freedom, honesty, community and courage as transcendent experiences: "In each such experience more than ourself or any part of ourself seems to be operative. . . . These experiences lead even the atheist to feel at moments as if he might be participation in the life of an other than he."[9] In *Man Becoming*, Gregory Baum is aware of the transcendent in the two dimensions which constitute human selfhood—dialogue and communion. Man comes to be through dialogue with others. Out of this ongoing dialogue a man develops a sense of who he is and where he is going. Men speak to each other words of acceptance and love but they also speak painful words that call for conversion and new life styles. For Baum in and through these human words a special word is spoken, a word which transcends the people involved. This word is discerned as transcendent and gratuitous because the speaker knows that it is not necessarily his alone and that by it he himself is judged. The same awareness is present in communion. Man in communion with other people is loved and accepted. In this love and acceptance he finds the strength to reply to the special word of conversion offered him. This love and acceptance which is the core of man's freedom is a gift given him by others. But here again man senses that the gift of human communion goes beyond it, transcends human ambiguity and frailty. Man knows that the gift dimension of life is more than he is. How a man becomes aware of a transcendent presence in human life is highly individual and rooted in each man's personal story. What is necessary is that an "ontological sensitivity" is developed for it is this sensitivity which supplies the meaningful context for religious symbolism.

[9] Michael Novak, "The Unawareness of God", *The God Experience*, ed. Joseph P. Whelan (New York, 1971), pp. 8, 15.

Although the religious symbol is born in a situation of transcendent disclosure, it does not merely mirror that situation. Transcendent situations, because of their intensity and the immediate recognition that they are of supreme value, are often experienced as ambiguous. In the face of this ambivalence the religious symbol "takes sides". It interprets and clarifies the transcendent dimension. A concrete example of the relationship between religious symbolization and transcendent awareness is Par Lagerkvist's *My Father and I*. A father and son are out for a walk on a Sunday afternoon. It was a beautiful day and their walk took them farther than they expected. Suddenly it was night and they were engulfed in darkness. In order to find their way they followed the railroad tracks. The father was calmly thinking to himself but the boy was filled with fear. The darkness was devouring him. He hardly "dared take a deep breath for then you got the darkness inside you and that was dangerous". The boy moving close to his father tells him that the darkness is horrible. The father replies:

"No, my boy, it's not horrible," he said, taking me by the hand.

"Yes, Father, it is."

"No, my child, you mustn't think that. Not when we know there is a God."

I felt so lonely, forsaken. It was so strange that only I was afraid, not Father, that we didn't think the same. And strange that what he said didn't help me and stop me from being afraid. Not even what he said about God helped me. I thought he too was horrible. It was horrible that he was everywhere here in the darkness, down under the trees, in the telegraph poles which rumbled—that must be he—everywhere. And yet you could never see him.

We walked in silence, each with his own thoughts. My heart contracted, as though the darkness had got in and was beginning to squeeze it.

Then, as we were rounding a bend, we suddenly heard a mighty roar behind us! We were awakened out of our thoughts in alarm. Father pulled me down onto the embankment, down into the abyss, held me there. Then the train tore past, a black train. All the lights in the carriages were out, and it was going at frantic speed. What sort of train was it? There wasn't one due now! We gazed at it in terror. The fire blazed in the huge engine as they shovelled in coal; sparks whirled out into the night. It was terrible. The driver stood there in the light of the fire, pale, motionless, his features as though turned to stone. Father didn't recognize him, didn't know who he was. The man just stared straight ahead, as though intent only on rushing into the darkness, far into the darkness that had no end.

Beside myself with dread, I stood there panting, gazing after the furious vision. It was swallowed up by the night. Father took me up onto the line; we hurried home. He said, "Strange, what train was that? And I didn't recognize the driver." Then we walked on in silence.

But my whole body was shaking. It was for me, for my sake. I sensed what it meant: it was the anguish that was to come, the unknown, all that Father knew nothing about, that he wouldn't be able to protect me against. That was how this world, this life, would be for me; not like Father's where everything was secure and certain. It wasn't a real world, a real life. It just hurtled, blazing, into the darkness that had no end.

The father and son are caught in the same potentially terrifying situation of being "lost in the dark". The father perhaps because of an inherited traditional response is quickly "at home", reminding himself that the unknown is God. It seems the son realizes the transcendent overtones of the situation more intensely than the father. For him the darkness is its own interpretation. It encompasses, terrifies and threatens him. Life has no preferences. It is coldly neutral which is the most insidious form of hostility. Life just "hurtled, blazing, into the darkness that had no end". The story makes clear the possible ambiguity of the transcendent dimension of experience. Is life ultimately a mad, rampaging train indifferent to each man's fate or is it concerned and supportive of the human person? Confronted with this ambiguity the Christian symbols do not passively reflect it but actively interpret it. They intuit this ultimacy as gracious and call it God. But no matter what answer a man gives to this question, the awareness of the question itself is the beginning of religious symbolism.

IV. The Second Naïveté

The quest for a second naïveté is a pastoral reality at the heart of Church life. Men and women passionately want their inherited religious symbols to speak to them of the sacred—to assure them, to critique them, to call them. For this to happen in the modern world a man must understand the contributions and limits which the cultural mood—a complex blend of science, psychology, sociology and history—bring to the expression of his faith. Most importantly he must recover a sensitivity to the transcendent dimension of his experience which is the birthplace of religious symbols and their eventual referent. Although it is necessary, it is not enough merely to understand the function and meaning of religious symbols. A risk must be taken. A man must live within a constellation of symbols and allow them to interpret and guide his life. This is what the surrender of faith means. The truth of a symbol, its adequacy to experience, can only be known from within. To verbally acknowledge the existence of God can remain a matter of intellectual conviction: to live within the symbol of God is a matter of existential life style. A man who lives within the symbol of God experiences the world as gracious. Despite his fears and anxieties, despite the possibility of tragedy, he finds a source and a power that enables him to act beyond himself, to celebrate and to sacrifice. His centre is within yet beyond himself in the transcendent otherness of his experience and this centre "will hold".[10]

[10] See W. B. Yeats' "The Second Coming":
> "Turning and turning in the widening gyre
> The falcon cannot hear the falconer;
> Things fall apart; the centre cannot hold."

PART II
BULLETIN

Eugene Kennedy

Religious Faith and Psychological Maturity

FAITH is a concept which has many definitions. For the purposes of this article I will consider it as a function of the human personality which reflects and expresses the pattern of convictions through which an individual views the ultimate significance of his life and the meaning of the universe around him. It is intimately related, then, to the qualities of personality fostered by social and cultural forces as well as by theological teachings. Man is inherently a believer; he seeks for explanatory myths to make sense out of his experience. The character of the beliefs to which he commits himself seems closely related to the kind of person he is. Although we are far from sophistication in measuring the element of faith through the techniques of social science, the evidence that we do possess suggests that the maturity of faith is dependent on or strongly conditioned by the individual's overall personal development. This raises as many questions as it provides answers.

This conclusion, however, is in harmony with the thrust of contemporary theology which has been marked by a return to man and an effort to rediscover and describe more accurately the unity of his experience. Faith is not a static entity, a gift bestowed in finished form at any one point in an individual's life. It is as much in process as is the personality of the individual who believes. Faith runs through the personality as the bloodstream does through the body; it not only gives life to the person but it is also affected notably by the overall health of the individual. Man the perennial believer simply cannot be divided up according to the fashion that allowed us once to speak of faith as a restricted operation touching man's intellect or will. Faith is more pervasive than that and must be considered in relationship to the total presence of an individual in life. To over-simplify for the moment, the less a person grows to his own individuality the more hampered he will be in developing his religious faith. On the other hand, the more fully human a person becomes, the more capable he is of exercising a vibrant, searching and satisfying religious faith. Religion has suffered a twin kind of difficulty for many generations. Viewed by social scientists and medical specialists it has often seemed a neurotic disorder, the manifestation of the search for magical solutions to life's difficulties, or the gropings of persons who had never satisfactorily resolved their parents. That is the kind of religion that can rightly be classed as the opium of the people. On the other hand, ascetic theologians have been as unkind to religion in quite another way. They heavily mortgaged it, making its highest expressions and experience the property of persons who seemed to disown or detach themselves thoroughly from their own human experience.

Mysticism became the function of the well-keened psyche, the final triumph of the person who had vanquished the body in the name of spiritual glory. Both of these views have made it difficult to look at religious faith as an aspect of the normal healthy personality. The research that has been prompted by the theoretical work of the late Gordon Allport over the last generation has done much to restore a sense of balance about the place of religion in life. No longer need it be thought of as the product of neurotic distortions nor need it be conceived of, in its highest form, as the exclusive property of over-spiritualized mystics. History is filled with the traces of man trying to talk to himself about the meaning of his life; his myths have reflected for us his efforts in every age to preserve, in a singular way, the epic themes which enable him to understand himself and his life. Just as it is natural for man to dream, so it is natural for him to believe, to have dreams of another sort, the dreams which give him an explanatory vision which he can keep safe from the ravages of time and to which he can return for sustenance and support as he tries, in each generation, to face the tasks that challenge the quality of his manhood and his faith. The tasks cannot be separated: man evolving as an individual and as a species seeks a richer and deeper grasp of his own identity and that of the world he has been given to tend.

Allport suggested that religious faith could be conceived of on a continuum, the poles of which could be labelled intrinsic and extrinsic.[1] Allport distinguished between these contents by identifying intrinsic religion as a master motive through which an individual is able to organize and understand all the experiences of his life. Intrinsic faith, in Allport's view, is a well-developed and mature kind of religious belief. On the other hand, however, extrinsic religion represents the compartmentalized and quite external form of religious behaviour which has no roots in the individual's personality. Far from being that through which the person is able to judge his actions and guide his life, extrinsic religion is a utilitarian and instrumental phenomenon which he uses to fulfil obligations, allay fears and to hold on to for the sake of his own salvation. This is the religion of the immature or underdeveloped person whose other outlooks and convictions parallel the shallow quality of his religious orientation. In further research, for example, Allport sought to demonstrate that racial prejudice was frequently found among people who could be described as extrinsically religious; it was not found in subjects judged to possess a more mature religious outlook.

Essentially, extrinsic religion represents a non-integrated value, the significance of which is grasped only superficially and the effects of which are found minimally in the way a person directs his life. It is closely akin to the religion of childhood, an unquestioned inheritance which is accepted on the authority of those who instruct the individual in its tenets. It never moves much beyond this in the life of the extrinsically religious person. The maturely religious person, however, passes through a crisis of belief in which he questions what he has received from others in order to test it against what he has learned from his own experience. Some persons abandon religious convictions of a formal

[1] Gordon W. Allport, *The Individual and His Religion* (New York, 1950); *The Nature of Prejudice* (Cambridge, Mass., 1954; "Religion and Prejudice", in *Crane Review*, 2 (1950), pp. 1–10; *Personality and Social Encounter* (Boston, 1960); "The Religious Context of Prejudice", in *Journal from the Scientific Study of Religion*, 5 (1966), pp. 447–57.

sort at this time of crisis in their life, sometimes because the fundamentalistic beliefs in which they were reared no longer seem adequate to explain the universe or their knowledge of it. Others turn back from the crisis to hold on to the faith which seems endangered by previously unthinkable questions. The growing person, however, accepts the challenge of self-examination and transforms his faith through a process of internalization at this stage of life. Now he believes for himself rather than on the authority of someone else. The outcome of developed religious faith is quite parallel, in Allport's design, to the self-responsible characteristics of the mature individual who judges his own experience in the light of the evidence which he is able to procure for himself.

This conceptualization of religious faith enables us to understand it as a developmental problem. As such, it is no different from any other developmental problem of human beings. They can, after all, be challenged by crises for which they are not prepared; their general development can be arrested by a complex of social forces and pressures; they can advance into the mature years of life with the psychological equipment of an adolescent. One must look beneath the appearance in order to discover the true psychological state of the individual within. Religious faith seems to be correlated with the other developmental processes; it does not operate independent of them. Although Allport's schema has been subjected to an array of technical and theoretical criticism, it has proved durable and, in the words of Professor James E. Dittes, it shows a considerable promise of surviving its obituary.[2] Most of the research which has employed the intrinsic-extrinsic paradigm has tended to support Allport's general outlook. Indeed, a recent survey of the priests of the United States, conducted through the psychological department of Loyola University of Chicago, addressed itself, in part, to the quality of faith of the subjects of the investigation.[3] The results of this study demonstrate the richness of Allport's conceptualization as well as the developmental nature of religious faith.

[2] "Intrinsic-Extrinsic and Church Sect", in *Journal for the Scientific Study of Religion*, 10, 4, pp. 375–84.
[3] Eugene C. Kennedy and Victor J. Heckler, *The Loyola Psychological Study of the Ministry and Life of the American Priests* (1971).

In conjunction with the other instruments and extensive interviews carried out during the pilot projects and actual study, a special maturity of faith scale was developed which enabled the researchers to make judgments on whether the developmental level of the faith of the respondents reflected their overall personal development. The main body of the research made it possible to assign American priests to various categories reflecting the stage of their psychological development. These were labelled the *maldeveloped*, the *underdeveloped*, the *developing*, and the *developed*. In the maldeveloped category are those persons who, although still functioning in the priesthood, give evidence of serious and chronic psychological problems which have interfered in a marked way with their personal and professional lives. The underdeveloped do not manifest such serious difficulties; rather, they reflect a failure or inability to come to terms with the adult challenges of psychological growth. They are considered underdeveloped in that their psychological age does not match their chronological age. Although they look adult, and have adult responsibilities, these men have generally failed to resolve the tasks which a man must face in the adolescent stage in his life. The developing group comprise individuals who, although they had been arrested in their growth for a time, have begun to grow again and to deal with the unfinished business of their personal development. There is much energy in this group, a clearly dynamic cluster of individuals for whom the pursuit of unfinished growth became the most important business of their lives. The developed group of priests represents the individuals who have dealt successfully with the various stages of their life, have developed their capacities well, and who, although not absolutely perfect, represent what we understand by psychological health.

In those aspects of the research which investigated religious faith, it is fascinating to observe the gradations of faith which seem to follow closely on the subjects' levels of personal development. The *maldeveloped* show the greatest number of characteristics of extrinsic faith. The *underdeveloped*, while more advanced than the *maldeveloped*, still evidence more signs of extrinsic faith than either the *developed* or *developing* groups. Interestingly enough, the priests in the *developing* group manifest a slightly higher index of intrinsic religious faith factors than do those in the *developed* group. All of the groups, however, are more intrinsic in their religious faith, in a statistically significant way, than the *maldeveloped* group of subjects.

Why would the *developing* group seem at least equal to the *developed* group in the nature of their intrinsic religious faith? The answer is probably connected with the fact that they are more vitally involved in dealing with their psychological growth, more excited about it, than any of the other groups in the study. While relatively complete integration of personality is obviously a desired stage of development, the rediscovery and pursuit of this seems to activate a person's energies in a quite remarkable way. This is also evidenced on another psychological test, the Personal Orientation Inventory, on which the developing group scored more highly than any of the other groups. To come psychologically alive is a process which has profound effects on all of a person's behaviour. It seems, in other words, that when a person shakes off the lethargy of arrested personal development the intensity of the experience is reflected in some way in everything he does, including the way he scores on psychological tests. There is an exuberance which reflects the dynamic of growth that has been re-engaged. It is not surprising to find individuals who could be classified as *developing* slightly more intrinsic in their orientation than even the *developed*. They are presenting themselves with questions for which they previously thought they had the answers and they are, in some sense, enjoying the ambiguity of the experience. It is still difficult for them to test the nature of their religious faith and to peer into their own psychological adjustment, especially if this has been embarrassingly preadolescent. There is, however, a remarkable positive trust in human persons through which they move themselves forward when they have at last come in contact with the real heart of their own life experience. There is an overflow, a sense of feeling alive, that accompanies discovery of new depths both in oneself and in one's faith. The data of this study support the general concept that the quality of an individual's religious faith is inseparably related to the level of his psychological development. Faith does not stand alone, or outside the personality; it is something that we understand only if we understand the persons who exercise it.

Several questions arise in the light of these findings. First of all, one can lay aside the contention that religious faith is merely a neurotic outcropping. It is clear that the deepest and most functional religious faith is a property of the individual who has the best sense of himself, his own powers, and his purpose in life. People who believe maturely also relate to themselves and to their neighbours maturely. They have dealt with the questions of life which mark man off as separate from the other orders of creation. With authentic awareness they have learned some of the lessons of loving, the highest expression of which has always been conceded to represent the highest operational definition of religious faith. This is not to deny that neurotic religion can exist; it manifestly does in the lives of many persons whose needs give shape to the world they inhabit. Their faith generally reflects something about their overall adjustment: as a man is, so he seems to believe. There is nothing startling in this, although it is refreshing to find evidence to support it. Secondly, mysticism cannot be the exclusive property of people who, in some arduous fashion, have overcome the body in order to live almost exclusively the life of the spirit. This is to make the richest expression of religious faith a function of the dis-integrated personality. We may have to look much more carefully at our discussions of mysticism and asceticism. Good balance and good judgment, a good sense of relationship to others: these are accepted as signs of psychological adjustment and it is difficult to imagine that they should be absent in the life of a person who lives by a deep and lively faith. What is truly mystical may, in other words. be present in the intensity of life of persons who are psychologically well adjusted. They are able to love and trust others deeply; they have a sense of possession of themselves and a capacity for entering into life in a profound way. Mysticism may be made up of such experiences rather than of the extraordinary and sometimes seemingly bizarre behaviours with which it has often been described. Mysticism, in other words, is found in the heart of human experience rather than at its remote and inaccessible edges. Perhaps we have overlooked the healthy kind of adjustment that seems to be present in the lives of great figures such as Teresa of Avila and distorted what seems to be other than this. Many people resist this interpretation of profound religious behaviour, finding it too prosaic and too unromantic. None the less, if religion and healthy personal growth go hand in hand, then we must put mysticism back into a more realistic psychological perspective.

Thirdly, it is clear that the unity of human experience is attested to by both Allport's theory and the cited research. Man cannot be effectively divided into separate spheres, even in the name of religious faith. It is difficult to find a dividing line in the human personality according to which we can set the sacred on one side and the secular on the other. It seems no longer profitable to maintain the old distinctions of mind and body and flesh and spirit which crystallized the antagonisms which estranged man for so long from a proper sense of his own unity. The emerging religious consciousness of our time turns man back to himself, to the task of feeling again the oneness of the personality given to him by God. One can no longer suppose that the religious man searches for a spiritual order that is separate from his own human experience. The unity of life in a totally redeemed universe must be reasserted in order to heal the wound from which man has suffered because of the exaggerated dualism that has disembodied the things of the spirit for such a long time. Man cannot be approached only on the spiritual plane. He must be approached as man. Religious categories must be capable of being discussed in terms of human experience in order to end the estrangement which history has introduced into man's sense of his own personality.

Fourthly, serious questions with implications for everything from catechetics to the liturgy must be asked in view of the relationship between full personal growth and a well-developed religious faith. The reason is clear: most people do not possess a fully developed personality and do not have a fully developed religious faith either. Those who are alive psychologically and religiously may be close relatives to the individuals who are categorized as *developing* in the study of American priests. They are, in a respected ascetical phrase, *"in via"*. They understand that the Christian journey is one of growth towards a goal which they have not yet achieved. The excitement lies in the possibility and promise of the goal, in the conviction that it endures against the ravages of time and space and in the commitment to the experiences which bring human beings closer to it. Is it impossible, one might ask, for a severely neurotic person to have mature faith? It may well be, but it is not impossible for a neurotic to have a maturing faith. If the Christian life is a dynamic, process-oriented experience built on the unitary nature of personality, then these ideas need not estrange us from traditional positions. Indeed, one might return to the history in ascetic literature in order to rediscover the images of growth which have always pervaded it. The understanding that man is made to grow and to fulfil a destiny that is at once religious and personal is hardly a new idea to anyone who has ever read the New Testament.

David Tracy

The Religious Dimension
of Science

I. Science and Religion: Their Relationship

IT IS now clear that the centuries-old dispute between "religion" and "science" is largely past history. Except for fundamentalists in both fields the emerging consensus is so clear as almost to have become a cliché: both fields have their own specific data, methods and languages. The disputes from Galileo through Darwin are tragedies unlikely to be repeated. The somewhat desperate moves of some religious thinkers to find "gaps" in scientific theories for the now discredited "God of Gaps" to enter are in widespread disrepute. Correlatively, since the emergence of the literally non-imaginable theories of modern physics the mechanical models of classical scientific theory no longer need refutation by troubled religious humanists.

The present relationship between science and religion, however, is far more complex. A whole range of issues have emerged in the natural and human sciences which bear considerable impact upon the study of religion. And yet—with a few notable exceptions—the attitudes of a La Place or a Freud or T. H. Huxley seem curiously dated. For the present situation is more correctly described as a search for the significant similarities and differences between the scientific and the religious dimensions of man.

Many perhaps most contemporary scientific and religious thinkers hold for some variation of what might be labelled the "two-language" approach to this question.[1] On the one hand

[1] Cf. Ian Barbour, *Issues in Science & Religion* (New York, 1966), pp. 115–25.

many linguistic philosophers argue that religious language is "participant" or "self-involving" language (Austin, Evans) in a manner which scientific language as "spectatorial" cannot be. On the other hand, most religious thinkers influenced by neo-orthodox theology hold to their own variation of the "two-language" approach. Karl Barth, as the clearest exponent of this variously articulated position, held that theology is concerned only and solely with "revelation" and is therefore neither encouraged nor distressed by the "neutral" discoveries of science.

Indeed, despite the demise of both neo-orthodoxy and the earlier versions of linguistic philosophy, the "two languages" approach to the question of religion and science probably still remains the majority opinion among thinkers in both disciplines. Still for a growing number of thinkers the "two-language" approach to the question of the relationships between science and religion, however comforting to both groups, is not really an accurate description of the relationship. For several recent thinkers argue that there are, in fact, significant similarities between the two disciplines. So much is this the case that many thinkers are willing to argue not only for the scientific study of religion (a commonplace) but also for the "religious dimension of science" itself. The intent of this brief article, then, is to examine that latter and more recent claim. For if that claim is true it surely promises a bright future for the close interdisciplinary work of all scholars upon the host of specific problems which the present and especially the future hold.

As a first generalization, it seems fair to state that most thinkers who hold to some version of this latter "mediating" position are philosophers and theologians with a good grasp of contemporary scientific methods and conclusions.[2] Indeed whether their philoso-

[2] The works referred to include the following: Ian Barbour, *Issues in Science & Religion, op. cit.*; *idem* (ed.), *Science & Religion: New Perspectives in the Dialogue* (New York, 1968); Bernard E. Meland, *The Realities of Faith* (New York, 1958); Schubert M. Ogden, *The Reality of God* (New York, 1966); Bernard Lonergan, *Insight. A Study of Human Understanding* (London, 1958); *idem, Method in Theology* (New York, 1972); Michael Polyani *Personal Knowledge* (Chicago, 1958); Langdon Gilkey, *Religion and the Scientific Future* (New York, 1970); Louis Dupre, *The Other Dimension* (New York, 1972); Stephen Toulmin, *An Examination of the Place of Reason in Ethics* (Cambridge, 1950); for an instructive study of

phical position be one of process philosophy (Ian Barbour, Bernard Meland, Schubert Ogden) or transcendental method (Bernard Lonergan) or general reflection on the nature of scientific method (Michael Polyani, Langdon Gilkey) or phenomenology (Louis Dupre, Paul Ricoeur) or even linguistic philosophy (Stephen Toulmin), all conclude to what may be interpreted as a "religious" dimension to the scientific enterprise itself.

It is true, of course, that many cultural factors are operative here. The gradual and steady re-emergence of'the positive need for symbol and even myth has rendered earlier discussions of "demythologizing" in accordance with the prevailing scientific world-view not so much incorrect as incomplete. The recurrent pattern of technological and ecological crises have rendered the curiously optimistic and manipulative "end of ideology" discussions of the 1950s as dated as other cold-war rhetoric of that period. Indeed, most parties to the present discussion—theologians, scientists, philosophers of religion and philosophers of science—are by now somewhat chastened in their former self-assurance. They have learned the lessons of the tragic relationships of the past as well as the legitimate demands of the more recent "two-language" approach. They have learned to be careful to articulate the significant differences in methods and data in science and theology before approaching a question like the "religious" dimension of science itself. Moreover, there is a growing consensus among such thinkers on the need for a discipline like metaphysics to mediate the cognitive claims of any horizon-factor labelled the "religious dimension" of science.

Such, in outline form, are some of the principal factors which render the present situation notably different from either the "science vs. religion" disputes of the past or even the "two-language" approach of the very recent anti-metaphysical neo-orthodox and linguistic hegemony on this question. But rather than provide yet another survey of the shared conclusions of these different "mediating" thinkers, we might best understand that conclusion by interpreting the argument of one major participant in the discussion, the Canadian philosopher and theolo-

---

the historical relationships of "religion" and "science" cf. Hans Blumenberg, *Die Legitimität der Neuzeit* (Frankfurt, 1966), esp. pp. 75–201.

gian Bernard Lonergan.[3] One can, I believe, best understand his argument by clarifying certain concepts and their relationships step by step.

II. THE RELIGIOUS DIMENSION OF SCIENCE:
FIRST STEP: SELF-TRANSCENDENCE AS SCIENTIFIC AUTHENTICITY

The central categories involved in Bernard Lonergan's analysis of what I have called the religious dimension of science are the linked concepts of "self-transcendence" and "limiting questions". The major reason for the choice of "self-transcendence" as the central category (as distinct, for example, from "self-fulfilment") is clear and, I believe, sound. For one lives authentically in so far as one continues to allow oneself an expanding horizon. That expansion has as its chief aim the going-beyond one's present state in accordance with the transcendental imperatives, "Be intelligent, be reasonable, be responsible, develop and, if necessary, change". On the simplest level, man transcends himself first by his sensitivity. For as a sensitive being, like all the other higher animals, man is related not merely to himself but to all the realities about him. Yet man does not possess only the habitat of the animals. He also lives in a world of meaning, a "universe".

For Lonergan, we understand this self-transcending possibility best when we reflect upon our ability to ask questions, especially scientific questions. For scientific questioning impels one past an experienced world of sensitive immediacy to an intelligently mediated and deliberately constituted world of meaning. In so far as we ask and answer questions for intelligence—Is it clear? What is it?—we learn to understand and unify, to relate and construct, to generalize some view of the whole. In so far as we go on to ask and answer questions for reflection—is it so? why? for what reasons? by what criteria? with what force of evidence? —we learn to affirm some reality beyond ourselves, our desires,

[3] As students of Lonergan's thought will note, the analysis serves as an interpretation rather than paraphrase of Lonergan's own position. For example, Lonergan's more traditional formulation of our question as "the question of God" is reinterpreted in the more contemporary context of the "question of a religious dimension of science". Further, the conjunction of the concepts "self-transcendence" and "limit-questions" is interpretative. I trust, however, that the very brief analysis remains a legitimate reformulation of Lonergan's position.

needs, fears, and even acts of understanding. For we learn, in our judgments, to affirm an unconditioned "yes" or "no" a fact, a reality, a truth not constructed by our own needs but demanded by our critical intelligence. We learn that the real world is constituted not only by our experiences of sound and taste and sight and hearing and touch of what is "out-there" nor only by our desires and fears and needs and feelings for what is "in-here". Especially for the scientist, the "real world" is also constituted by what we understand and affirm with evidence. For example, we literally cannot imagine the theories of quantum mechanics. But we can understand and affirm them. Such scientifically probable judgments, it is true, only allow for a *cognitive self-transcendence*. Yet the fact demanding clarity is precisely that scientific judgments really are examples of such cognitive self-transcendence. In a word, they are objective. For such judgments are the inevitable and critical products of our own self-transcending subjectivity.

Ordinarily, however, we do not remain satisfied with a merely cognitive self-transcendence. We are not, for example, prepared to allow technology to develop unhampered by consideration of ethical factors. Except for "Dr Strangelove" or Adolf Eichmann types, most scientists and technologists are determined to find ways to act and live in accordance with critically determined values. We cannot but raise questions of value for our deliberation, evaluation, decision and action. And in so far as we answer these questions of value in a critical manner we know that we are again involved in self-transcendence. For we have decided for what is truly good and not merely for what gives us pleasure and helps us to avoid pain. We know, then, when and how we have moved past a level of merely cognitive self-transcendence to one of real, moral, existential and communal self-transcendence.

III. The Religious Dimension of Science:
Second Step: Self-transcendence and the Question of God

It is also to be noted that the increasing complexity of the scientific drive for self-transcendence from sensitivity through intelligent and critical reflection to deliberate action also manifests certain transcultural factors in the scientific enterprise itself. Indeed the questions for intelligence, for reflection, for deliberation so clearly involved in science can be labelled genuinely transcendental notions. Such notions are transcendental precisely in so far as they are recognized to be the very conditions of the possibility of being an authentic human being. To understand them as such, to be sure, requires an extended exercise in transcendental reflection (as Lonergan himself attempts at length in *Insight* and more summarily in the opening chapters of his recent *Method in Theology*).

For present purposes, however, it will be sufficient to reflect upon certain widely shared demands for continuing self-transcendence in the scientific community itself in order to understand the character of the question of God in that context. The facts of everyday good and evil, of scientific, technological and ecological progress and decline do eventually give rise to questions about the basic character of this universe for the authentic scientific inquirer. For unless he wishes to abandon the search for authentic self-transcendence the scientist cannot silence the question of the final horizon of scientific inquiry itself. On the contrary he may reflect upon each level of self-transcending inquiry to understand what horizon or dimension it presupposes. First, on the level of questions for intelligence the authentic scientific inquirer can inquire into the very possibility of fruitful inquiry. In his scientific research a scientist can and does reach intellectually satisfying answers. Yet he can also ask such "limit-questions" upon all inquiry as the following: could these answers work if the world were not intelligible? could the world be intelligible if it did not have an intelligent ground? In other words, once he has reflected upon the conditions of possibility of his own inquiry, the scientist may find himself face to face with the ultimate religious question, the question of an intelligent ground for intelligibility, the question of God.

On the second level, the scientist can reflect on his scientific judgments as distinct from his intelligible hypotheses. In Lonergan's own vocabulary, the scientist may reflect upon his ability to reach a virtually unconditioned affirmation, i.e., a conditioned whose conditions happen to be fulfilled by scientific evidence. Yet he may also note that each virtually unconditioned judgment reached is not the ultimate ground of itself or other such judgments but merely one case of such. Scientific judgment, to repeat, is a conditioned whose conditions happen to be fulfilled to a high degree of probability. Hence the scientist might also ask whether there can be any virtually unconditioned judgments unless there exists also a formally unconditioned (i.e., an unconditioned in the strict sense of no conditions whatsoever). Once again, then, the scientist may be driven by his own critical intelligence to ask a question of a final or grounding horizon for all his judgments.

On a third level, the scientist can deliberate about his own need to evaluate his findings in accordance with ethical values. At this point, the scientist (especially here the human scientist) may well ask: Is it worthwhile to ask whether our goals, purposes and ideals are themselves worthwhile? Can we understand and affirm such a demand for worthwhileness without affirming an intelligent, rational, loving source and ground for them?

It might be noted that since the question of God is here expressed in terms of the commonly available transcendental notions the question itself is not imposed extrinsically but is rather well within the scientific inquirer's own horizon. That question is the final dimension of his own inquiry. In fact, the scientist can deny the need for such limit-questions into the intelligent, rational and responsible grounds of the scientific enterprise only at the unwelcome price of self-contradiction. For no inquirer can commit himself to the task of authentic self-transcendence (i.e., intelligent, rational and responsible thought and action) and then deny his own need to seek the ultimate intelligent, rational and responsible grounds of such action. At precisely that point the scientist may, as Stephen Toulmin reminds us, elevate some scientific theory (e.g., evolution or entrophy) to the level of a "scientific myth" wherein the theory may now function as an ultimate (i.e., religious) dimension for existence itself. But short of self-contradiction the scientist cannot fail to recognize reflectively the need for some such dimension however he may wish to label it. If he admits that possibility, the scientific inquirer can no longer rest satisfied merely with a "two-language" approach. Rather he will attempt to mediate that final or ultimate dimension either symbolically or mythically or philosophically. In all such mediations, he may well find that such a final horizon or dimension precisely as ultimate is legitimately interpreted as religious.

It is true, of course, that Lonergan's own analysis depends upon his transcendental method for its mediation. Yet, although I am myself convinced that Lonergan's method is fundamentally sound on this point, I am by no means reluctant to have the same argument mediated by other and quite different philosophical approaches. Although present space does not permit an extensive analysis of them the fact remains that other philosophical positions also mediate a recognition of a "religious dimension or horizon" of science. For example, either Louis Dupre's Hegelian phenomenology or Alfred North Whitehead's process philosophy or Stephen Toulmin's linguistic analysis of the "limiting questions" in science all mediate such an understanding. Toulmin's analysis, for example, is particularly helpful in mediating that logically distinct and prior domain of fundamental reassurance and confidence in the worthwhileness and intelligibility of our existence which is the logically peculiar character of all our religious assertions and the logical presupposition of all scientific and ethical inquiry.

In summary, just as the "existentialist" rediscovery of the category "limit-situation" helped to mediate a recognition of the peculiar character and necessity of religious meaning for humanists, so a careful study of the category "limit-questions" to scientific inquiry can mediate a recognition of the authentically religious dimension of that most human of enterprises, contemporary science. Neither theology nor science, then, has anything to fear from a future collaboration which recognizes the autonomy and the mutual interrelatedness of these two sorely needed conversation partners for our critical present and future. All they have to lose by such dialogue is the memory of their past tragic history and the unpromising spectre of a future non-conversation between a dehumanized science and a ghettoized theology.

Rosemary Ruether

The Messianic Horizon of
Church and Society

THE biblical message was a political message, in the sense that it did not divide the individual from the community, the sacred from the secular or the spiritual from the corporeal, but its message was addressed to the people in history. The ultimate *telos* of human history is not "other worldly", in the sense of a flight to heaven which leaves the present world unchanged, but rather points to the ultimate grappling with the systemic disorder of the world itself that will overcome this and bring creation into harmony with God's will. In the Lord's Prayer, "heaven" stands as the mandate for what should be done *on earth*, in order for God's Kingdom to come. But the prophetic message was not "secular politics". Such a distinction between politics and God's will, or between ethics and politics, belongs to the modern schism of consciousness. The prophetic message was the "politics of God". God's word was the mandate and demand within which the struggle for an authentic social order was carried out and from which vantage point it was judged. The messianic promise led Israel into a revolutionary politics which, for three centuries, engaged in guerrilla struggle against the great imperial powers of Rome and Greece. The Apocalypses, written from the time of the Maccabees to the Jewish Wars, were the literature of this resistance movement.

But messianic politics are not the only kind of religious politics. Conservative as well as radical social movements have implied a religious sanction and world view. In classical societies indeed there was no political order which did not place its political system within the framework of a cosmic and divine order as its ground and source of being. The king was the visible embodiment and representative of the divine King of the universe. Jewish and Christian messianism did not sever this relationship between religion and politics, but rather challenged the myth that this integration between God's Kingdom and the kingdom of man is already achieved. But this declaration of a disharmony between the two rests on the assumption that the two should be in harmony and ultimately will come together in harmony on the other side of "God's revolution".

The myth of Christendom was built on a partial appropriation of this future hope. God's reign was seen as already established through the establishment of the worship of Christ and the "defeat of the demons" of pagan idolatry. A new integration of God and empire was declared, proclaiming the emperor or the pope as the new "vicar of God's Word on earth". When this myth of Christendom began to break down in the modern period, leading to the liberal revolutions of the nineteenth century, this did not dispel the religious dimension of politics. Rather it released its messianic dimension to act again as a revolutionary horizon for the human historical enterprise. Christendom and the Church now found themselves assailed with the same antagonistic myth with which they had once assailed the pagan empire. Now they were the "Leviathan"; the "Dark Ages"; the superseded humanity that was to be replaced by the dawn of the new age of Light. Religion and the transcendent, having been squeezed out of their vertical relationship with society, were being smuggled in again as the transcendent horizon of the new historical project that was to go on from "glory to glory" to the final perfection of man in society.

Just as the old religious world views, whether messianic or ontocratic, revolutionary or static, implied a politics, which either blessed the present social order or decreed divine judgment against it, so now the new politics and practice of progress contained a hidden theology which was the more evocative because its metaphysical content was largely unacknowledged. This unstated messianic theology, which looked forward to a new horizon of integration of man and God in the transcendent *telos* of historical progress, would cause generations of men to pit themselves in furious struggle against social systems painted in diabolical colours. It could also be turned around to give a halo of messianic blessing to the new revolutionary societies created out of this struggle that were now presumed to incarnate the basis of this perfection, even though the completion of the "divine mission" still lay in the future. The revolutionary party thus recaptured the infallibility and aura of divine vicarship once claimed by popes and kings by divine right. The very "secularism" of these regimes became a way of absolutizing these presuppositions in a way that put the premises beyond question. One-dimensional secularity, therefore, has acted less as a denial of an absolute, as an incorporation of it into the bases of the present system in a way presumed to guarantee the fulfilment of man's highest hopes.

In his provocative book, *Christianity in World History*, Arend van Leeuwen argues that the Christian myth of messianic hope, secularized as the technological thrust of Western, post-Christian societies, is now extending itself from the West to uproot and transform all traditional ontocratic societies into that messianic culture of revolutionary struggle and world-transforming future hope that was implanted in history by Christian revelation. The apocalyptic Christ is, after all, the "centre of history", as traditional Christian salvation history believed. But Christ is the centre of history, not in the sense of a straight-line conquest of the world by societies called Christian or an institution called the Church, but in a dialectical manner, by which all humanity realizes its historical character by appropriating the secular content of the Christian paradigm of messianic humanity. But this can happen only in an antagonistic relationship with the ecclesiastical and Western power structures that carried this gospel. At precisely the point where the sacralizing walls of the Church and Christendom dissolve, the inner content and dynamism of this messianic myth is becoming the myth of universal human salvation. Now all humanity sees life as a revolutionary struggle against established power structures and a world-transcending élan towards a New World.

Van Leeuwen fails, however, to reckon with an important historical fact about the roots of the messianic myth. He assumes that the messianic myth is the opposite and anti-thesis of the myth of divine kingship of sacral societies, instead of seeing that the idea of the Messiah is precisely this same myth of divine kingship appropriated by Israel from its Canaanite neighbours. The word "Messiah" was originally the throne name of the Davidic king. And the ecstatic, transcendent dimension of messianism was this transcendent dimension of kingship ideology, ever disappointed in actuality, projected upon the future. This is why messianism, both in its Christian form in the Church and in its secular, revolutionary form, far from being proof against sacral societies, has constantly reproduced them! Ontocracy and apocalypse have been corollaries in Western history. This is surely why the myth of the divine Kingdom and the myth of the world-destroying apocalypse have tended to appear, fatefully, together in modern revolutions. This may also be why the drive to build a new world where all men's hopes will be satisfied tends to go hand in hand with a technology of death that can only end in the happening of that fiery "end of the world" that was once only the despairing dream of a seer. The question before us then is not merely the vindication of the relevance of the messianic myth to modern revolutionary man, but whether we can break the fateful nexus between the polarities of this myth in time to prevent the death wish of the Warfare State from cancelling out the benefits of the Welfare State.

I would argue that the messianic horizon is properly understood in relation to society, when it is neither fused with society nor merely opposed to society, but stands in a constant tension between the proximate horizons of man's possibilities and the ultimate horizon of God's possibility. This is also the meaning of the distinction of Church and society, which must become neither a fusion into Christendom, or yet a separation into the "other-worldly" church which demonizes the "world". When the Church fuses with society, then messianic hope is imported into the basis of society to absolutize it. The same effect takes place in revolutionary societies when the revolutionary "party" establishes itself in power as the fulfilment and sole source for the achievement of "The Revolution". This is the reason for that peculiar similarity, which has often been noticed, between Catholic and Marxist Constantinian states. On the other hand, when the Church declares that its future hope is purely "other worldly" and irrelevant to society, it gives up its critical function in relation to society. This acts either to validate the *status quo*, or else as a demonizing of society that gives birth to its opposite in a new sacral society, when the messianic counter-culture overcomes the present society and sets up a new one in its place. The Church keeps its proper role in relation to society, not by defining itself as a "separate people" with a hope that is unrelated to a demand laid upon society and creation, nor yet simply selling out to bless the bombs of the political *status quo*. Rather the Church keeps the messianic horizon in its true relation to society by standing at a critical distance from every society, in order to act as that ever-renewed prophetic edge of society itself, that stands for the tension between man's works and God's demand. But it does so precisely in order that this messianic horizon can act as a vantage point for both judgment and for renewed aspiration in society itself.

This "double horizon" of temporal and ultimate future hope, that appears whenever one tries to discuss "salvation", points to that unknown border between man's actual possibilities and that transcendent possibility of God, which appears to be "beyond man's nature", and yet which something "in his nature" still demands as the "still more" of his fulfilment. This is the unknown border which we cannot define because we do not know what is possible. This is the horizon of the world where reality is unfinished and its nature is not determined, but is still in process of being created. Here is where messianism broke the closed ontocratic concept of Being towards the Becoming of a universe exploding into the future. Yet this "still more" cannot be simply against or contrary to creation, but must itself be the realization of a demand which God implanted in creation "from the beginning". Otherwise saved man would be unrecognizable to himself, instead of affirmed in his deepest and truest being. This was the purpose of the classical Christian Christology which identified the Christ of the Eschaton with the Logos through which the world was created.

The inability of any theology or cosmology or political ideology to complete this circle without contradiction is the measure to which our thinking itself must remain incomplete, as the world itself is incomplete. The paradoxical tension between the "orig-

inal" and "eschatological" poles of the messianic myth is illus-
trated by the development of the ancient Hebrew myth of Exodus
into the later apocalyptic myth of the "end of the world" and the
angelic "new Creation". The myth of Exodus might well be seen
as an anti-eschatological myth. It is the story of the escape from
that Egypt which subordinates man's real daily life to the building of the pyramids of mummified death. The escaped slaves flee
from thanatocratic absolutism to return to finitude in that "local
space and time" which is where man can find a "home and a
land of his own". Were Philo and the Church Fathers correct
when they infinitized this myth so that it became the story of
the flight of the soul from the body into the eternal, immutable
heaven? Or did this not contradict the redeeming direction of
the original myth, which pointed away from self-infinitization
and back to real historical existence? Anti-utopian myths of
"return home" to local space, time and identity appear redeeming when men have wandered too long in absolutizing expectations which have all proved disappointing. Yet the homeland
that is gained never satisfies. Even the Jewish Passover tells us
that "even if we were in Jerusalem, we would still have to say
'next year in Jerusalem'", for the present Jerusalem is not the
fullness of the Jerusalem of hope.

The contradiction of human hope, then, is this; the destiny to
which man is called is not one which annihilates him, but recon-
ciles him to his truest nature, yet he can find no vantage point
for this simply by returning to any original starting-point that
has existed in history. This is because "nature" is not a *datum*,
but a process still being born from chaos. But this is also because
man's shaping of that process has misshapen it so that it now
partakes as much of man's alienation from his destiny as it does
of the proper nature of that destiny. For this reason man's flight
from the Pyramids of Power exists in a symbiosis with that self-
absolutization which creates the Pyramids of Power, so that imperial oppression and apocalyptic revolt tend to oscillate as two
sides of the same urgency.

The history of modern utopias, kakotopias and science fiction
nightmares expresses this same contradiction in the language of
that hope generated by technology. Modern ideologies of progress and revolution suggest the myth of an infinite exodus to

that ultimate fusion of man with the absolute *telos* of history. Marxist apocalypticism, as well as Hegelian progressivism, assumed that there was an "ending-point" in history which is, at the same time, the "end of history" and the fusion of history with a transcendent goal. Teilhard de Chardin's Omega point of cosmic evolution put this ideal into the larger framework of natural evolution. The theology of hope boldly declares that "God is the future of man"; i.e., the word "God" means the infinite future potential of man. Yet these absolutizing dreams suddenly become nightmares when we see what megamachines of absolute power are being built up upon the earth out of these expectations! What does Teilhard de Chardin's Noosphere sound like, literally, if not the great computer of 1984 in which individual thought and creativity has been subordinated to a centralized master mind of the totalitarian State? This affinity of the messianic human imagination for totalitarianism makes ancient ontocracy reappear in the form of the world pentagon of power, as Lewis Mumford has pointed out in his two volumes on ancient divine kingship and modern totalitarian states (*The Myth of the Machine* and *The Pentagon of Power*).

Over against these myths of exodus into infinity, we have the anti-utopian myths of anarchism, liberalism and crisis theology, and even Camus's philosophy of rebellion. Each, in different ways, revolts against the tyranny of the Absolute, as man's governing identity, and points back to finitude as the creaturely context of man's authentic life. Anarchism does this by revolting against the absolute State and pointing back to the idealized, self-governing, peasant village. Liberalism would also reject the absolute State in favour of limited and divided public power. Crisis theology saw the very essence of man's sinfulness as his rejection of his finitude for self-deification. The "Wholly Other God" became a rod to break man's heaven-storming élan and return him to earth to live day by day with repentant mind. Camus also pointed man back from his revolutionary flight into the absolute future to his real ground in the present, to live in unperfectible solidarity with his fellow man and his finite mother, the earth. Yet these anti-utopian myths are redeeming only in their clash with absolutism, but they find no resting-place in the present. They tend to become stultifying, therefore, to the extent that they ideologize the *status quo* as "the best that we can expect".

Thus man's goal remains a mystery because man's nature is unknown to himself. Classical Christology of the Logos-Messiah was intended to provide a perspective on this situation by lifting our eyes beyond the existential paradox to the larger ground on which man can stand that, alone, can give him the surety that his future is meaningful. Only the One who "will be" because he "is" and "was" "in the beginning" can remove us from the tyranny of lifting ourselves by our own bootstraps to heaven, and can give us the courage, not only to exodus constantly against debasing situations, but also to live day by day in inconclusiveness without losing faith, hope and love.

René Laurentin

The Persistence of Popular Piety

IS traditional piety doomed in the "secular world", as Bonhoeffer
and Bultmann thought? Or has it been given a new chance at a
time when festivity and gratuitousness are making a comeback
in forms such as the writing of Harvey Cox or the clowns of
Godspell?[1]

The aim of this article is not to give a theoretical answer to
this question,[2] but to illustrate it by a typical case, that of the
Lourdes pilgrimages, which stem from the apparitions of the
Virgin Mary to Bernadette (11 February–16 July 1858). I have
chosen this particular example for the following reasons:

1. It is indisputably an example of *traditional religious* piety,
whatever meaning is given to those ambiguous words.

[1] Harvey Cox, *The Feast of Fools* (Harvard, 1969, and London, 1970).
Godspell is a celebration of the Gospel in mimes by clowns of the utmost
seriousness, which translates into action the ideas of Cox's book.

[2] The wording of the question put to me illustrates an ambiguity in
current language. "Traditional" in current usage normally means a "tra-
ditionalist" attachment to recent, decadent forms, inherited from the recent
past of the Counter-Reformation. In its true meaning, however, the word
stands for Tradition with a capital "T", the living transmission of the
Gospel. Lourdes fits the first sense, as a Marian pilgrimage started in the
middle of the nineteenth century, but it also fits the second, as a genuine
resurgence of the great motifs which introduce the Gospel, poverty, prayer
and penance, and the joyful atmosphere of the message brought to Mary.

"Religion" can be understood in the sense of the *religiosity* which Barth
contrasts with *faith* (and in this sense Christianity is not a religion). But
it may also mean the reference to the meaning and salvation which are
essential to human life which Tillich has called interest in "ultimate concern".

2. Lourdes combines a range of important religious phenomena, apparitions, a holy place and sanctuary, pilgrimage, the
celebration of the sacraments (the Eucharist, penance, the anointing of the sick), prayer and various rites, classical or peculiar to
Lourdes, the rosary, singing, processions, offerings and candles,
the use of water as a drink, an ointment or for washing in a new
form of John the Baptist's "baptism of repentance".[3]

3. A last reason for the choice is the vitality of Lourdes. Even
on the level of statistics, the number of pilgrims has never ceased
to increase. The million visitors a year was reached in 1908, half
a century after the apparitions, and the two million, passed on
two exceptional occasions, 1954, the Marian Year, and 1958, the
centenary of Lourdes, has been kept up since the latter date. The
three million was passed in 1964, and the 1971 total of pilgrims
was 3,362,525 (see the table at the end of this article).

Nor is this an isolated case. Comparable numbers can be found
in the pilgrimages to Guadaloupe in Mexico, Aparecida in Brazil,
Fatima in Portugal, etc. There are about a thousand sanctuaries
which receive more than 100,000 pilgrims a year. It is in view of
the size of this phenomenon that the author of this article has
devoted a considerable part of his work to this field, which is
too often neglected or treated with disdain by theologians.[4]

We shall examine in turn two key points:

(1) the objections which depreciate this phenomenon of traditional
piety, and
(2) the efforts and progress towards evangelical authenticity made
at Lourdes.

[3] 107,229 men and 260,821 women bathed in the (icy) pools of Lourdes
in 1971 (*Recherches sur Lourdes* 37 [January 1972], p. 30). This rite takes
on a new relevance as the Jesus movement and its derivatives multiply
collective baptisms.
[4] R. Laurentin, *Lourdes. Documents authentiques*, 7 vols. (in collaboration with B. Billet for vols. 3–7) (Paris, 1958–1966), retraces the history of
the pilgrimage by means of original documents; *Lourdes, histoire authentique des apparitions*, 6 vols. (1961–1964), is a critical history of the eighteen
appearances of the "Immaculate Conception" to Bernadette; *Logia de Bernadette* (Paris, 1971) is a critical study of Bernadette's words; *Bernadette
vous parle* (Paris, 1972), 2 vols., is the story of her life; *Pontmain, histoire
authentique*, 3 vols. (Paris, 1971), is a historical and theological study
made for the centenary of the shrine.

I. The Criticisms

The authenticity of Lourdes has been challenged with varying degrees of force, not only by Protestants but also by Catholics from committed groups, for the following reasons:

1. Is not the search for graces and cures at Lourdes part of a magical or centripetal attitude which is opposed to the centrifugal movement of authentic religion?

2. Is not this form of piety sentimental and emotional? Is it not a form of collective euphoria or simply the herd instinct which crowds people together wherever there are the most people, whether it is at entertainments, on beaches or in supermarkets?

3. Do not these pilgrimages encourage inward-looking rites? In 1967 the figures for a pilgrimage from Northern France showed that 65% of the pilgrims were non-practising.[5] These pilgrims seemed quite happy to perform a whole marathon of religious practices at Lourdes, Masses, processions and rosaries from morning till night; they like to say, "We did everything". But when they go back home they return to their previous negligence. In such a case is not the pilgrimage an alibi, an escape, and is not the sanctuary an evil place which soothes the religious unease which ought to be kept alive until the moment of a real, lasting conversion?

4. And does not the concentration of the heavens which "opened" for Bernadette during the apparitions distract pilgrims from earthly realities, from the involvements in which the real salvation of men is worked out, the relations of justice and charity which are the presence of God?

The answer to these objections is theoretically simple. In itself there is no reason for a contradiction between interest and disinterestedness, emotion and faith, ritual and charity, heaven and earth. Genuine Christianity creates a balance in which the religious appetite is transformed into the gift of self, faith integrates sensibility, eschatological hopes stimulate earthly commitment, and sacramental rites foster love.

It is, however, a fact that this equilibrium is rare and pre-

[5] Dumesnil Report, submitted to Rome, 1967; *Recherches sur Lourdes* 21 (January 1968), p. 40.

carious. "I am not proud of my ministry here", I was once told by a Latin American religious. He had just been appointed rector of a sanctuary of Our Lady of Lourdes, set up on the model common in those parts: huge crowds of people coming, one day a week, to touch or kiss a statue and pay their money.

Deviations in the direction of supernaturalism, pietism, formalism, or even magic and superstitition are not the invention of the critics. The prophets of Israel long ago attacked religious fervour which did not "loose the bonds of wickedness" and abandoned widows and orphans (Is. 58. 6–8; cf. 1. 10–17; Zech. 7. 6–11).

For a long time Lourdes replied to objections with an aggressive and self-righteous apologetic. For a number of years recently, however, the authorities of the shrines have taken note of criticisms made by "a certain number of Christians engaged in apostolic activity" which criticize the pilgrimages.

—for being marginal in the Church;
—for going against the current direction of pastoral work, ... in a specifically religious context taking Christians out of their normal environment;
—for creating a transitory and artificial community outside normal life.
[Conclusions of the congress of pilgrimage directors, Rome, 1967, *Recherches sur Lourdes* 21 (January 1968), p. 41.]

They certainly do not accept the radical criticism which questions the value of any ritual or liturgical activity on the ground that the only "liturgy" of any value is political commitment in the secular world, but they do admit that the critics wish to improve the position.

As a result of this, the shrine authorities have undertaken a renewal of their pastoral work based on close attention to the fundamentals of the faith and the realities of life.

1. For about fifteen years the pastoral work of Lourdes and many other shrines has been governed by the following principles. Apparitions and private revelations must be recognized as having a purely relative value. They cannot add anything objectively new to the revelation of Christ. Their contribution belongs to the area of hope rather than that of faith. Their function is to

embody, at a specific place and time, neglected aspects of the Gospel. The more particular "messages" of apparitions must therefore be interpreted by the essential message of Christ.[6] Their function is to make that message present here and now, and refer us back to it.

These traditional principles, deriving from Benedict XIV, were fatal to the particularisms which emphasized the local, the special, the extraordinary aspects of the pilgrimage. This doctrinal reorientation completely undercut the aggressive mythology which ranged the apparition of the Immaculate Conception at Lourdes against the occult forces of freemasonry, rationalism and even "Protestant Germanism".[7] Lourdes is no longer in any way a refuge for French chauvinism.

2. This is no prefabricated pastoral care, but attention to a life, a life which is part of a history. This history is now known more accurately and more critically since the centenary: at the beginning the unlooked for event of the apparitions of 1858, the holiness of Bernadette which spoke directly to the common and obscure condition of faith and made her life itself the bearer of the gospel message of Lourdes—poverty, prayer and penance. We know all about the initiative which came from the poor people of Lourdes and created a pilgrimage before the hierarchy took it over. We can see better, not only the generosity, the prayer and the faith which have always been shown at Lourdes, but also the errors and excesses, big and small, the epidemic of visionaries whose fever tried to prolong the apparitions which had ended for Bernadette (10 April–12 July 1858), the craving for signs and wonders. (In the last century Père Picard, the founder of the national pilgrimages, had a dead body dipped into the pool and

---

[6] These principles were formulated in R. Laurentin, *Sens de Lourdes* (Paris, 1955), pp. 89–97, which was reflected in the Roman documents for the Lourdes centenary. They were republished in *Lourdes, histoire authentique des apparitions*, vol. 6 (1955), pp. 259–60.

[7] There is a collection of these early themes in *Recherches sur Lourdes* 37 (January 1972), p. 12, which includes the following hymn to Our Lady composed by the chaplain to the 18th Corps during the First World War and published in *Le Journal de la Grotte* 11 (14 March 1915), p. 3:

Un peuple en demence	Ils ont, horde impie,
Osa te braver.	Ri de ton pouvoir.
O Reine de France,	Toi seule, ô Marie,
Accours nous sauver.	Es tout notre espoir.

set the crowd praying to obtain its resurrection—the report of the scene fascinated Zola in 1892.)[8]

Even more than the lessons of history, what holds the attention of the association of pilgrimage directors and the Lourdes pastoral council is the immediate reality of the crowds which flow into Lourdes. The statistics are becoming more and more detailed: not only totals, but the different categories of visitors brought by road, rail and air, social background (54% of country people in the organized pilgrimages), age groups, etc.[9] Needs are identified and met. It was found that young people were relatively few, 12% between fifteen and thirty in the organized pilgrimages, and it was true that there wasn't really any place for them at Lourdes. An accommodation centre and a meeting-place have been set up for them.[10] Single pilgrims, who were for a long time ignored, are better received today: 60,000 were looked after in 1971.

II. Pastoral Progress

But the problem is not answering objections but showing in practice that the thing works, and the important question is therefore what progress the Lourdes pilgrimages have made towards fidelity to the Gospel.

Prayer and the liturgy at Lourdes have been renewed according to the spirit of the Vatican Council, and even beyond. From 1967 onwards, the Lourdes pilgrimages were used as a trial for a renewal of the "anointing of the sick", to give it a greater community sense and a sense of hope (Jas. 5. 15). The collective celebrations of this sacrament destroyed the old idea which made it an "extreme unction", the *last* gesture when there is no more hope. In 1970, two years after Rome had approved these experi-

[8] The statistics of the pilgrimages of 1951–1970 have been published in *Recherches sur Lourdes* 37 (January 1972), p. 48. See the table below, p. 155.

[9] This spontaneous development of the pilgrimage and its deviations are described stage by stage in *Lourdes, Documents authentiques*.

[10] This centre provides more than accommodation, and is intended to encourage meeting and discussion. It is run by a loosely organized group of young people. See *Recherches sur Lourdes* 37 (January 1972), pp. 39–40. All the aspects of the pastoral work done at Lourdes are covered regularly in this journal.

ments, the eighty-eight-year-old Cardinal Feltin was among those who received the sacrament at the grotto.

Since 1971 efforts have been made to emphasize the festive character of the pilgrimage, along the lines suggested by Harvey Cox. This was one of the conclusions of the last congress of pilgrimage directors.

These attempts have to feel their way. For example, in 1971 a first vigil with songs by John Littletown, organized to create the "festive style", won unanimous acceptance because it took place after the traditional torchlight procession and the transition had been carefully prepared. On the other hand, the replacing of the traditional closure of the rosary by a celebration in the form of a song recital in English by the same singer, with no introduction, was a failure, the lesson of which was immediately taken.

Lourdes is a place of creativity, above all in welcoming those who suffer and are excluded, especially the sick. They came spontaneously from the beginning. In 1874 the Langres pilgrimage, and then the French national pilgrimage, took the initiative of bringing them from a distance, on the primitive railway of the day: the challenge of the famous "white train" has proved beneficial far beyond the cures produced at Lourdes. The pilgrimage is a break in confinement, loneliness, in the monotony of these painful lives shut in with suffering. The pilgrims who come on stretchers find in Lourdes the example of St Bernadette, who was able to take up her "work of being ill" by reference to the cross and redemption of Christ. Their presence raises for the healthy a question about the meaning of their life and their death. And above all they stimulate kindly service in the spirit of Mt. 25. 39, 44: "I was sick, and you helped me." The Eucharist, which has always been at the centre of Lourdes, receives its full value and resonance as a result of this generosity, this communion with those who are making up in their flesh what is lacking in the sufferings of Christ.

In recent years, not only have the arrangements for visitors been improved both spiritually and technically, but new categories of sick have also been received; such as the annual pilgrimage of the blind (3,000), and the annual pilgrimage of polio victims, started in 1963. Even those in iron lungs are brought. Transporting them, and all the necessary equipment, has required great technical skill. More recently, the first pilgrimages of the mentally handicapped have taken place, with ceremonies adapted to their needs.

Other new developments have broadened the welcome of Lourdes to include groups suffering to various degrees from marginal situations. Gathered at Lourdes, the relatives of the handicapped are taken out of their anxious loneliness by meeting others who are undergoing the same trial, as in the picture in Isaiah 53. The pilgrimage of gypsies gives this nomadic people, the object of so much suspicion, the welcome and support of the Church as well as spiritual comfort.

The military pilgrimage may seem a shocking idea at a time when the qualitative changes in warfare is multiplying the grounds for conscientious objection, but it is not a militarist demonstration. It began as a challenge after the bloody Franco–German wars, by bringing together soldiers from hostile countries. Its aim is to be a meeting in peace and inner renewal and it includes soldiers of twenty nations who have been enemies in the past.

For twenty years constant efforts have been made to do something about the ugliness which had invaded Lourdes. Mgr Théas had the site scoured and the eloquent symbols of the grotto and the spring water restored to prominence. The *Lourdes 64* exhibition attempted to throw, if not a bridge, then at least a plank, between modern artists and the pilgrims. Painters and sculptors were invited to give free expression to the impression on them of what Bernadette said about the apparitions, what she called for a long time *Aquero*, "That"—a suggestive name for abstract art! The views of the pilgrims were sought on the works displayed at Lourdes, and it is interesting to record that the work of one of the best abstract painters of our time, Hartung, aroused a considerable response in this very mixed public.

The main concern of pastoral work is conversion, which has been from the beginning the major fact of Lourdes. As part of this concern Catholic Action opened, in 1958, the centenary year, the Lake Pavilion, to take advantage of the readiness of pilgrims to take stock of their lives.[11] The same concern today runs through

[11] Michèle Lesoeur, "Le pavillon du Lac et la pastorale de Lourdes", report dated 14 December 1971, in *Recherches sur Lourdes* 37, pp. 31-8.

all pilgrimages. "Preparing for after the pilgrimage" is one of the aims most heavily stressed by the local bishop, Mgr Donze.

The secular and material aspects of Lourdes have also been affected by this renewal. The economic sector was for a long time a struggle for survival between hotel-keepers and pilgrimage directors in search of the lowest prices. For the last six years there have been regular meetings of the hotel-keepers' and workers' associations to look at the question from the point of view, not of profit, but of human beings. The existence of trade unions has been recognized, and the first collective agreements in Lourdes were signed in 1971 (*Recherches sur Lourdes* 38 [April 1972], pp. 38–40).

The religious impulse of Lourdes is therefore not confined within the circle of a consoling ritual. It affects the human relations in which the justice and charity in which God dwells must be created.

III. CONCLUSIONS

The unique fact of Lourdes, with its imitations in similar pilgrimages both in the old world and in Latin America, invites the following conclusions.

1. It is not magic or running after miracles which keeps up the numbers at Lourdes, but a strictly religious impulse dominated by ideals of sacrifice and the desire to find a meaning in human life on the lines of what Tillich called "ultimate concern", beyond everyday determinisms.

A pilgrimage is an act which is first and foremost free, in the tradition of the Bible.[12] Following Abraham, the pilgrim leaves his house; for a time he abandons his habits and his personality and finds the freedom of the seventh day. The eschatological sense revives in him. The presence of the sick sharpens his awareness of the last things.

The freedom of the act of going on pilgrimage is shown by the fact that although the number of cures officially recognized at

Cf. H. Joulia, "Pastorale de Lourdes, rapport sur la vie des sanctuaires", *ibid.*, pp. 19–30.

[12] C. Spicq, *Vie chrétienne et pèlerinage selon le Nouveau Testament* (Paris, 1972).

Lourdes is tiny—no more than sixty-two since the beginning[13]—the sick continue to stretch the hospital services to their limits; the annual average in recent years has been 50,000. They come for something else, as is shown by surveys, from which we take some typical quotations:

"X, who came to ask for his own cure, begs for the cure of an invalid more seriously handicapped than he."

"Another invalid concludes more radically, 'How can you pray for yourself when there are so many suffering, so many war victims?'" (Surveys quoted by B. Billet, in *Recherches sur Lourdes* 37 [January 1972], p. 7.)

As far back as 22 August 1892, Emile Zola noted, "The most seriously afflicted invalids pray for their neighbours...a great sense of brotherhood...no jealousy" (*Mes Voyages* [Paris, 1958], p. 50).

The most important fact about Lourdes is conversions, not cures.

2. Does the numerical growth of Lourdes mean a rebirth of the religious sense? The problem can be formulated as follows. On the one hand, the less educated peasant sectors which made up most of the supporters of pilgrimages are declining, as is interest in miracles and the like. On the other hand, travel and tourism are favourable to pilgrimages. In what proportions to the effects of these two contrary factors operate? No serious study has yet given an answer.

3. The religious feeling which leads people to Lourdes is ambiguous. It may produce good or bad; it can be exploited, cheap-

[13] The claim that the number of miracles at Lourdes has steadily declined was first publicized by the pamphlet of T. and G. Valot, *Lourdes et l'illusion* (Paris, 1956). This assertion is, however, largely the result of a manipulation of irrelevant figures which are quoted simply to prove the authors' thesis. The statistics, on the other hand, show stability, when comparable figures are compared. Between 1946 and 1971 the Medical Bureau opened between 17 and 71 files a year (minimum in 1957, maximum in 1949). Slight variations are due in part to the increasingly strict criteria employed by the Lourdes international committee. During the period 1945–1971 22 "miracles" were officially recognized (varying between none, one and two a year). Before 1946 there was no official investigation, except in 1862, when 7 cures were recognized, and between 1905 and 1913 (40 cures recognized); these were carried out on less stringent criteria than those of today. See A. Olivieri and B. Billet, *Y a-t-il encore des miracles à Lourdes?* (Paris, 2nd edn. 1971).

ened, turned into a technique, alienation or superstition. But a religious appeal which makes demands, based on the Gospel, always finds a response among the crowd of pilgrims which brings to mind the "poor of Yahweh" in those "middle ranks of sanctity" to which Bernadette belonged even before the apparitions.

4. The often frustrated need for religion finds a response in the striking symbols of Lourdes. First the historical evidence of God's wonderful acts among his people, apparitions and miracles, then physical symbols which create a continuity with that history of grace, spring, grotto, mountain and gestures which bring nearer the presence of the living God and the communion of saints. Hence the popular formula which constantly recurs in the surveys: "Lourdes is a corner of heaven", "You feel you're no longer on earth", etc.

The pilgrim at Lourdes is also drawn into the life of a community brought together by a shared journey and common activity, prayer and the service of the sick. In this way faith finds an atmosphere in which it can breathe: "At Lourdes you can pray without looking a fool", was the comment of one teenager (*Recherches sur Lourdes* 37 [January 1972], p. 8).

This community is international in extent. Foreigners make up 43% of organized pilgrimages and about a quarter of the annual total of three million. Meetings at Lourdes are a real encouragement to the sense of brotherhood, of catholicity. Lourdes has even acquired an ecumenical dimension with the beginning of Orthodox, Anglican, even Moslem pilgrimages.

Pilgrims find at Lourdes the breath of prophecy in the sense of the making present of the impact of God in a specific, locatable time and place.[14]

5. If signs of this type did not exist in the Church today, they would have to be invented. The frustration engendered by preconciliar pastoral methods, which were too often abstract and administrative, produced, in compensation, an abundance of wild apparitions, not recognized and often suppressed by the Church,

---

[14] "We are suspicious of that prophetic mysticism which appeals to ... oracles from on high to award itself a mission ... in the Church and the right to wield influence there ...", Karl Rahner, "Les révélations privées", *Revue d'ascétique et de mystique* 25 (1949), pp. 506–14, esp. pp. 507–8.

LOURDES PILGRIMAGE—Statistics 1951-1970

Year	Total Special Trains	Special Trains (Abroad)	Planes	Pilgrims (Special Trains)	Pilgrims (Ordinary Trains)	Pilgrims and Tourists (Road)	Pilgrims (Air)	Out-of-season Visitors (various)	Total Pilgrims and Tourists	Hospital Cases (Seven Sorrows Hospice)
1951	416		140	249,600	630,000	650,000	1,051	101,349	1,632,000	24,224
1952	520	224	172	293,324	674,651	700,000	4,395	141,901	1,814,811	28,284
1953	345		224	216,909	399,224	500,000	6,250	210,480	1,332,863	25,725
*1954	670		854	392,229	907,390	900,000	25,527	350,921	2,596,891	33,580
1955	440	179	836	255,229	786,502	700,000	20,000	155,200	1,790,020	32,852
1956	472	184	811	279,239	651,692	700,000	19,600	150,500	1,801,031	33,065
1957	485	175	920	286,904	702,796	650,000	27,000	160,000	1,826,700	34,405
*1958	1,050	502	3,936	650,100	1,134,842	2,900,000	127,458		4,812,400	47,547
1959	535	247	1,595	303,004	697,020	1,147,757	52,219	150,000	2,200,000	36,737
1960	538	249	1,795	292,000	609,000	1,100,000	43,338	170,000	2,207,394	37,807
1961	558	256	2,931	331,877	848,308	1,260,000	62,698	170,000	2,672,883	40,826
1962	563	267	1,920	351,532	850,102	1,320,000	71,132	170,000	2,762,766	41,200
1963	597	281	1,935	407,387	887,460	1,350,000	84,595	170,000	2,899,442	49,250
1964	621	297	2,295	430,956	907,965	1,400,000	99,397	170,000	3,008,308	50,980
1965	608	275	2,573	434,853	907,510	1,420,000	108,221	170,000	3,040,584	51,802
1966	613	292	2,636	428,297	965,259	1,520,000	124,477	182,000	3,220,033	55,173
1967	625	295	2,671	387,087	969,539	1,420,000	149,859	170,000	3,096,478	53,135
*1968	533	239	2,270	321,135	1,043,335	1,150,000	112,382	120,000	2,746,853	48,119
*1969	574	261	3,167	354,762	821,324	1,500,000	152,541	185,000	3,013,627	49,821
1970	586	269	3,199	346,293	805,803	1,600,000	170,760	192,000	3,114,856	49,036
1971	616	297	3,636	394,002	802,458	1,750,000	218,065	198,000	3,362,525	44,731

* 1954: Marian Year; 1958: centenary of the apparitions; 1968: strikes in France in May and June; 1969: French Referendum, presidential election, strikes in Italy.
From the annual *Bilan touristique* of the Ville de Lourdes and the annual letter of the President de l'Hospitalité de N.D. de Lourdes.
Source: Recherches sur Lourdes 37.

but nothing seems to discourage the devotees. What they are looking for is a presence, a transparency, a breath of prophecy.[15]

6. At Lourdes religious feeling seeks an outlet with reference to the Gospel, with that ambiguous mixture of failure and success which characterizes all human effort. What is important is the vitality of the critical sense, of the demands of Christianity, and above all of creativity, not only in rites and signs, but also in their impact on life and human relations. The signs of Lourdes perform a quite subordinate function in leading the ambiguous aspirations of spontaneous religion to *agapē*.

In this matter the chief rule remains that of the Gospel, "You will know them by their fruits" (Mt. 7. 7–20; cf. 3. 10; 12. 23; 13. 22–23; Acts 5. 30–39).

[15] *Dossier des apparitions non reconnues, Cahiers marials* 77 (1 April 1971), gives a list of these religious phenomena for the period 1931–1971. There is a more thorough examination of the question (with a fuller list, 160 instead of 105 cases) in *Etudes mariales* 28 (1971). There is another list of 185 apparitions and similar phenomena in the brochure by W. C. M. Groos, *Veertig Jaar uit de Mariale Apocalyps. Een oriëntering*, supplement to *Op Doortocht* (October–December 1971), duplicated, Una Communitas, Postbus 5207, Amsterdam.

Translated by Francis McDonagh

Biographical Notes

GREGORY BAUM, O.S.A., was born in Berlin in 1923 and ordained in 1954. He studied at the University of Fribourg and at McMaster University, Hamilton, Canada. Master of arts and doctor of theology, he is professor of theology at St Michael's College, University of Toronto, and also editor of *The Ecumenist* and associate editor of the *Journal of Ecumenical Studies*. Among his published works are: *The Credibility of the Church Today* (1968), *Faith and Doctrine* (1969) and *Man Becoming* (1970).

JOAN BROTHERS was born in Liverpool in 1938, and studied at the University there. Doctor of sociology, she is lecturer in sociology at Goldsmiths' College, London University. She has given lectures on sociological themes (especially on the possible relation between sociology and theology) in many Protestant and Catholic institutions; she is engaged on the reclassification of ancient members of the secular and regular clergy; she has taken part in many ecumenical activities (particularly in dialogues arranged by the World Council of Churches). Among her published works are: *Church and School: A Study of the Impact of Education on Religion* (Liverpool, 1964), *Readings in the Sociology of Religion* (Oxford, 1969²), *The Uses of Sociology* (with J. D. Halloran) (London, 1966), *Residence and Student Life* (with S. R. Hatch) (Tavistock, 1971) and *Religious Institutions* (London, 1971).

ANDREW GREELEY was born in Oak Part (U.S.A.) in 1928 and ordained in 1954. He studied in the United States at the Seminary of St Mary of the Lake and at Chicago University. Master of arts, licentiate in theology, doctor of sociology, he is reader in the Department of Sociology at Chicago University and Senior Study Director of the National Opinion Research Center at the same university. Among his published works are: *The Hesitant Pilgrim: American Catholicism after the Council* (New York, 1966) and *A Future to Hope in* (New York, 1969).

BAS VAN IERSEL, S.M.M., was born in Heerlen (Netherlands) in 1924 and ordained in 1950. He studied at the Universities of Nijmegen and Louvain.

Doctor of theology, he is professor of introduction to Holy Scripture and New Testament exegesis at the University of Nijmegen. He is also chief editor of the review *Schrift* and a member of the editorial committee of the review *Tijdschrift voor Theologie*. Among his published works is *"Der Sohn" in den synoptischen Jesusworten* (Leyden, 1961).

EUGENE KENNEDY, M.M., is professor of psychology at Loyola University, Chicago. He recently directed the psychological study on the American priesthood for the National Conference of Catholic Bishops. He has written thirteen books, of which the last two were entitled respectively *The New Sexuality* and *The Pain of Being Human*. He has been consultant psychologist to a number of religious orders and dioceses and also to the Menninger Foundation of Topeka, Kansas.

RENÉ LAURENTIN was born in Tours in 1917 and was ordained in 1946. He studied at the Institut Catholique, Paris, and at the Sorbonne. Docteur ès lettres, doctor of theology, he is professor of theology at the Catholic University of Angers and teaches in many foreign universities: in Canada (Montreal, Quebec), in the U.S.A. (Dayton) and in Latin America, etc. He was consultor to the Preparatory Theological Commission of Vatican II, then an official expert at the Council. He edits the religious chronicle of *Le Figaro* (Paris). is vice-president of the Société française d'études mariales and also carries on a pastoral ministry in the neighbourhood of Paris. Among his numerous published works, many on questions of Mariology and on Vatican II, are: *Développement et salut, Nouveaux ministères et fin du clergé, Réorientation de l'Eglise après le troisième Synode, Lourdes: Documents authentiques* (6 vols.), *La Vierge au Concile, Jésus et le Temple, Dieu est-il mort?, Crise et promesse de l'Eglise aux U.S.A., Nouvelles dimensions de l'espérance*. He edits the Mariological chronicle of *La Revue des Sciences Philosophiques et Théologiques*.

NANCY McCREADY was born in 1943. She studied at Loretto Heights College, Denver (Colorado) and at Loyola University, Chicago. She obtained the B.A. and M.A. She was research assistant at the National Opinion Research Center of the University of Chicago for the Carnegie Project (evaluations of experiences in higher education) in 1969 and since 1972 has been a member of the Executive Bureau of the Cana Conference of Chicago. She is also a poet and has contributed to various reviews, notably *The New City, The Synergist* and *The New York Times Magazine*.

WILLIAM McCREADY was born in Evergreen Park, Illinois, in 1941. He studied at St Mary of the Lake Seminary, at Chicago University (M.A., 1966) and at the University of Illinois (Ph.D., 1972). Since 1971 he has been Associate Study Director at the National Opinion Research Center (Chicago). Among his works are: *Family Tension and the American Priest* (with Andrew Greeley), *Youth Culture and Occupation: Some Observations*, "American Catholic Pentecostals: A Social Analysis" and "National Sample Data on Religious Behavior: The Formation of a Data Bank" (report presented to the annual reunion of the Midwest Sociological Society, Kansas City, 1972).

MARTIN MARTY was born in West Point, Nebraska, in 1928. He obtained his Ph.D. at Chicago University in 1956. He is professor of modern history of the Church at Chicago University where he is also associate dean of the Divinity School, member of the Committee for the History of Culture and associate member of the Faculty of History. Member of the American Academy of Arts and Sciences and doctor *honoris causa* of seven universities, he has been president of the American Society of the History of the Church and is co-editor of the quarterly *Church History* published by that society. He is also editor of the bi-monthly *Context*, co-editor of *New Theology* and of *Ecumenical Studies in Church History*. Among his more recent books are: *Righteous Empire: The Protestant Experience in America, The Search for a Usable Future, The Modern Schism: Three Paths to the Secular* and *Protestantism* (in an international history of religion).

DAVID POWER, O.M.I., was born in Dublin in 1932 and ordained in 1956. He studied at the St Anselm Institute of Liturgy, Rome. Licentiate in philosophy and doctor of theology, he is professor of sacramental theology at the Gregorian University, Rome. Among his published works is *Ministers of Christ and His Church* (London, 1969).

JEAN REMY was born in Soumagne (Belgium) in 1928. He studied at Louvain University. Licentiate in philosophy and doctor of economic sciences, he is a professor at the Faculty of Political and Social Sciences at Louvain University and director of the Centre of Socio-Religious Research and of the Centre of Urban and Rural Sociology at the same university. Among his published works are: *La ville, phénomène économique* (Brussels, 1968); with F. Boulard, "Catholicisme urbain et pratique religieuse"—"Villes et régions culturelles. Acquis et débats" (in *Archives de Sociologie des Religions*, No. 29, 1970), and with F. Houtart three volumes of *Eglise et civilisation contemporaine* (Mame, 1968, 1969, 1970).

ROSEMARY RUETHER is a doctor of theology. She is professor of historical theology at Howard University, Washington, D.C. She has actively participated, in the last ten years, in movements in favour of American civil rights and of peace. She is the author of *The Radical Kingdom: The Western Experiences of Messianic Hope* which explains the relation of secularized Messianism in modern social movements.

EMILE SERVAIS was born in Leroux (Belgium) in 1939. Licentiate in political and social sciences (Louvain University, 1966), he is assistant to Professor Jean Remy at the Centre of Socio-Religious Research at Louvain. He is co-author with Francis Hambye of an inquiry into the cultural system of Louvain students, author of an analytical essay on religious discourse (cf. *Social Compass*, XVIII, 1971, 1) and co-author with Pierre Hiernaux of "Une expérience de pédagogie institutionnelle, réflexions, critiques sur certain aspects de la méthode", in *Recherches sociologiques* (Louvain, 1972).

JOHN SHEA teaches theology at Niles College, Loyola University, Chicago. Fr Shea is author of two books—*What a Modern Catholic believes about*

Sin and *What a Modern Catholic believes about Heaven and Hell*—and of numerous articles in the reviews *New City, The Critic* and *The Ecumenist*. He is at present engaged in research into the relation between human experience and religious symbols.

DAVID TRACY is a priest of the diocese of Bridgeport, Connecticut, and a doctor of theology of the Gregorian University, Rome. He is associate professor of philosophical theology at the Divinity School of Chicago University. He is the author of *The Achievement of Bernard Lonergan* (1970), contributes to several reviews and is editor of the *Journal of Religion* and of the *Journal of the American Academy of Religion*. He is at present engaged on a book on fundamental theology.